PRO TACTICS™

BASS

PRO TACTICS™

BASS

*Use the Secrets of the Pros to
Catch More and Bigger Bass*

Karen Savik

THE LYONS PRESS

Guilford, Connecticut

An imprint of The Globe Pequot Press

TO MY HUSBAND AND DAUGHTERS,
WHOSE PATIENCE AND SUPPORT HAVE ALLOWED ME
TO PURSUE MY TOURNAMENT FISHING DREAM.

To buy books in quantity for corporate use
or incentives, call **(800) 962–0973**
or e-mail **premiums@GlobePequot.com.**

The Lyons Press is an imprint of The Globe Pequot Press.
Pro Tactics is a trademark of Morris Book Publishing, LLC.

All interior photos by Mitch Kezar, Windigoimages.com

Text design by Peter Holm, Sterling Hill Productions

Library of Congress Cataloging-in-Publication Data is available.

ISBN 978-1-59921-297-5

Printed in the United States of America

10 9 8 7 6 5 4 3 2 1

CONTENTS

ACKNOWLEDGMENTS

Many people worked hard to make this book possible, and I'd like to dedicate some space to thank them. For starters, my mom and dad raised me to appreciate and care for Mother Nature. I firmly believe that all anglers (or any outdoor user) should be responsible stewards for the environment, and I owe that sense of responsibility to my wonderful parents, Gene and Virginia Jenniges.

Next, if it hadn't been for my big brother, Steve Jenniges, who loaned me the money to enter my first tournament circuit as a pro fifteen years ago, this book probably never would have happened. It took me three years to pay him back, but I never would have become a hard-core tournament bass angler without his initial financial support. I had a short window of time to tackle this sport professionally, and had it not been for Steve, it wouldn't have happened for me.

My husband of twenty-seven years, Ken, and my daughters, Britta and Kirsten, deserve so much credit for their patience and support in understanding my passion for fishing, even though they don't necessarily share it. Their constant encouragement kept me going when the chips were down (and up), and when I'm on the road, I always know they're "taking care of business."

Thanks also to all the professional and amateur anglers who shared my boat or competed against me over the years. I've learned something from all of you, and you forced me to improve and play up to your incredible level. You've been great friends and made me a better angler. All my sponsors have made it possible through great products, equipment, and financial sponsorships to participate in the wonderful sport of tournament angling. Ranger Boats, Land O' Lakes, Evinrude, Lowrance, Abu-Garcia, Fenwick, Berkley, and MinnKota have been great sponsors to represent on the water and at shows and events across the country. The wonderful people at these companies have become friends for life!

On the publishing side, thank you to Tim Lesmeister and Rob Drieslein for their guidance and assistance in putting my thoughts and ideas to paper. And photographer Mitch Kezar deserves massive kudos for making this book so visually enticing: He snapped all the great images you see. He made me look good!

Finally, to the public reading these pages, thanks for your support. I'm living proof that anybody can make it in bass fishing and share his or her experience with others. Don't let any obstacles stand in the way of your doing the same!

Why Me, Why Bass?

What's an Upper Midwest girl doing writing a book about bass fishing? Well, my fishing career started back in my childhood when I simply wanted to spend some time with my dad. Like many Minnesotans, he fished for walleyes but—again like many Minnesota anglers—usually caught pike. The only lures I knew were Lazy Ikes, Dardevles, and Red Eyes! We didn't even own a boat. Once my dad caught a bass, though, and from the first time I laid eyes on a tough bigmouth flipping and flopping on shore, I knew I wanted to learn more about these special fish. With their big eyes, shovel-pail of a mouth, and colorful bodies, these fish intrigue Americans of all sizes, ethnicities, and economic backgrounds, and they truly impressed that little girl from Minnesota.

By my teenage years, I—admittedly—was more focused on socializing and chasing boys, so my fishing got a bit sidetracked. Eventually I married my husband and began raising a family of my own. We weren't wealthy, but we made time for summer lake cabin vacations with our daughters. Those trips were great fun, and they resparked my interest in chasing bass. Wherever Americans travel, there's a bass lake nearby, and I believe that explains a lot of the appeal of bass fishing nationwide.

Bass bid fair to qualify as the nation's number one sportfish because they're virtually ubiquitous and a trophy for men and women from either side of the tracks—the common person's muskie or tarpon. You can enter the sport at your own pace and spending level, or you can eventually—like me—make bassin' a passion and lifestyle. Living in Minnesota, I certainly found ample access to great bass fishing within minutes of my house. This was also the time that catch-and-release was a growing fishing phenomenon, especially among bass anglers, so my timing was perfect: Bass populations in much of the country, particularly in my region, were improving, thanks to the simple fact that fewer stringers of big fish were being brought home.

I bought my first boat at age thirty-eight, and by the time my kids were teenagers, I had become a serious bass fisherwoman, eventually entering the fishing tournament scene in 1994. I started as an amateur co-angler, but—call me a control freak if you want—I felt like I was fishing with one arm tied behind my back. Co-angling was frustrating for me, and I realized, fast, that I wanted my own rig. After fishing the Minnesota-based Silverado series, I won my first event, the 1997 Minneapolis Aquatennial Bass Championship on Lake Calhoun, by flipping the milfoil with a jig-and-trailer. That was a real thrill: winning a tournament on a lake that I had grown up swimming in and topping other anglers whose names I'd admired for years in the Twin Cities area. It was a turning point for me. I suddenly realized that I was as capable of winning an event as anyone else launching a boat. I was hooked, so to speak.

Since the mid-1990s I've traveled around the country, fishing events as a full-time bass tournament fishing professional, first on the Minnesota Pro-Am Bass Tour and then, for most of this decade, on the FLW Tour. That's not unheard of for a woman, but to this day there still are just a handful of women who put on the kind of miles on their boat and trailer that Karen Savik does year after year.

People shake their heads in disbelief at my lifestyle. What is it about bass fishing that puts me on the road twenty weeks per year, sometimes in brutal weather conditions? Some walleye writers love to slam unworthy bass and bass anglers with all our gear, gussied-up boats, and wild-eyed approach to our outdoors pursuits. When I encounter walleye-loving curmudgeons, I usually just reply, "I'd rather not fall asleep when I'm fishing." (No kidding; I hear all the time about guys falling asleep while they're walleye fishing! Must be the fumes from all that backtrolling, eh?)

But why does a baby-boomer girl whose contemporaries are hosting wine tastings and hitting the theater or opera spend most of her free time either preparing for, traveling to, or participating in bass-fishing extravaganzas? It's not all for the money, as many successful pro anglers usually break even or make only a few bucks via tournament fishing.

It's because I just love it, plain and simple. My brother lent me money to fish my first pro tournament series, Minnesota's Silverado, and I still remember my first event vividly. I caught one fish, but it was the greatest feeling ever. For a while during that event, I thought more than once, *Why am I doing this?* Then I caught that fish and said, "Yeah, that's why!" In the following pages I hope to convey why bass fishing means so much to me and how easily bass fishing can become a wonderful part of your life, too.

There are plenty of books that explore bass-fishing techniques and opportunities in the southern portion of the United States, but in this book

The support of sponsors allows tournament anglers from around the country to enjoy their bass-fishing passion professionally.

I want to share some of my insights that come from chasing largemouth and smallmouth bass all across the country. Most of that experience came via chasing northern bass, which in my opinion don't receive the respect they deserve from most of the nation's elite bass chasers. It's true: We don't enjoy the growing season that allows those southern, or California, "hawgs" to grow so large, but we do have tens of thousands of beautiful clear-water lakes that support robust bass populations. No, you're not likely to catch a 10-pound Wisconsin or New York largemouth, but I know many lakes where I can catch lots of 4-, 5-, and 6-pound largies. If that idea intrigues you, then keep reading. There's a lot to learn about bass, and in terms of access, both the northern United States and the South offer great bass waters. Many of my tournament pals started out shore fishing for bass, including yours truly, so there's no reason any person reading this book can't seriously consider entering the sport.

I'm still a tournament-fishing girl (writing this book between spring 2007 tournaments hasn't been easy!), but I haven't lost my love of fishing for fun. If I work the night shift at our family business, you'll often catch me heading out midmorning to a fantastic lake about twenty minutes from my home. Too often, I'll have a fabulous morning of fishing all by myself, look around and say, "Gosh, I wish someone was here to share this!" Sharing my love of fishing is almost as much a personal passion as the actual fishing, which is a major reason I embarked on the challenge of writing this book. So grab a gunwale and prepare to learn about serious bass fishing. I love this sport, and when I'm done telling you about it, you will, too!

Opposite: The author with a chunky "largie." Bass are an extremely accessible species of fish in the United States for people of all ages, genders, and income levels.

Very few people in the Lower 48 don't live within a few minutes, or at most a couple of hours, of a waterway that can produce bass like this.

CHAPTER ONE

Meet the All-American Fish

Unlike some fish, a few of which I consider downright ugly, largemouth and smallmouth bass are muscular, handsome species. Millions of people fish bass because they're found across the United States (and beyond). Like people, they're active during the day, smart, and they have a big appetite, so—unlike those finicky finesse gamefish like walleyes or trout—you don't need a degree in angling-ology to pursue them. Did I mention they're loads of fun to catch? They tussle like spunky streetfighters, barreling toward the bottom after the hookset, leaping out of the water like few other freshwater species, then shaking their heads vigorously at boatside.

That's not to say the sport is "fishing in a barrel," so to speak. Bass have responded well to catch-and-release and better angling techniques during the past decade, too. Wherever I fish them, bass can handle respectful handling, a picture, then—with a flick of their tail—they bolt back out of sight. Bass are the all-American fish: They like a good tussle, live life a million miles an hour, and can thrive in places other creatures ignore. Must be why I like them so much!

Peruse the Florida-based International Game Fish Association's recordbook, and you'll see that many species of gamefish—saltwater, freshwater, and from other continents—share the name "bass." Striped bass and white bass also can be found in fresh water. I've fished stripers in Beaver Lake, Arkansas, and have many friends who've fished them off the East Coast. By whatever name, they're a rocking good time to fish. That's a topic for another book, however. For the purposes of these pages, I'm going to focus on the two black bass species most anglers think about when talking about bass fishing: smallmouth and largemouth.

Like their more southerly cousins, such as spotted bass, these species belong to the sunfish family (per the IGFA recordbook), which fish biologists call the Centrarchidae family. That's about as scientific as I'll get in these pages, but I think it's important to share that fact so that anglers understand that in one respect we're ultimately just pursuing big panfish. Little three-to-a-pound bluegills can put up a pretty good fight. You've seen them bend your son's or daughter's Snoopy pole a time or two, I'll wager. Well, imagine a 2- or 3-pound bluegill. Quite a tussle would ensue, right? So go figure that a 3- or 4-pound bass can put a hurt on your biceps when you're hauling him in! Understanding bass biology will help us in many ways later when we plan tactics and search locations.

Bass and Their Environment

Even through they live in a very different environment from people, smallmouth and largemouth bass alike rely on senses that are pretty understandable to those of us who breathe air. A quick Web search reveals that there's been a lot of research into fish vision, and scientists say bass indeed can see in color. (That's reassuring to those of us who purchase all those bizarre-colored lures to catch bass. Glad it's not just a big marketing ploy, right?) Thumb through a fishing catalog and you'll see lures representing all colors of the rainbow. Those colors may rarely exist naturally underwater, but they exist in my tackle box! I have no clue why such colors perform, but they do. In an effort to present heavily fished bass with new patterns, some modern fishing lures combine flash, translucent colors, and even glowing elements.

In turbid spring or river water, all fish rely more on their sense of smell or lateral line to locate prey.

My tournament schedule usually takes me to turbid lakes during the spring-runoff season or to rivers, where water clarity usually is pretty marginal. Here's where our knowledge of the bass's lateral line and other senses pays off. The lateral line is that faint exterior line of dots on the outside of virtually all fish. It helps them—almost sonarlike—to detect movement and vibration in the water. You'll hear fishing gurus at seminars or on radio broadcasts talk about the need to keep crankbaits and other lures properly tuned, and the lateral line is the big reason why. A well-tuned lure delivers more vibration and pulse to the water—vibration that fish will detect (and, we hope, pursue) thanks to sensing it via that lateral line. Make sense? (No pun intended.)

In these more turbid areas, where bass use their vision less to find and strike my lures, I can work the scent and noise factor to my advantage, too. You'd better believe I have rattle presentations ready for such conditions. Also regarding the noise factor, any self-respecting angler can tell you that noise scares any fish species, so I always make a conscious effort to remain as quiet as possible. People have been trying to entice fish via their sense of smell for thousands of years, and so-called high-tech, modern bass anglers are no different. My fishing experience has taught me to take the smell factor seriously, and in a tournament situation, I'll try anything that might give me an edge. Even if scented products like salt-impregnated or garlic-scented lures help enliven my bass fishing just a smidge, it's worth a shot! Also, I keep my hands as clean as possible and avoid any unnatural scent or human odors that might alarm the fish.

Locating Bass

Part of the appeal of bass and bass fishing is that these fish can inhabit so many regions and types of waters. Contacting state natural resource agencies is the quickest way to determine if a body of water near you contains largemouth or smallmouth bass. Many agencies provide lake

profile data with contour maps on their Web sites where you can quickly search which species are present. Private businesses also sell lake maps that delineate clear structure, GPS coordinates, and other data that can help streamline your search. The ability to research a lake or river thoroughly before even hitching up your boat and trailer has advanced light years since I began tournament fishing. If you enjoy traveling to new destinations to catch bass, there's no better—or easier—time than the present, thanks to the volumes of information quickly and affordably available in the digital age via software and the Internet.

If you want to search specific lakes or rivers, it's easy. But in this section, I'd like to break down some basic trends that hold for bass locations across the northern tier of the United States. Let's start with the simple lake. I'm no geologist, but a little research explains the history behind the abundance of water in the Upper Midwest, Northeast, and southern Canada. The last ice age ended 10,000 years ago, and the massive sheets of ice that covered the northern United States left all sorts of geological features scattered across the landscape. States like Wisconsin celebrate this geological past with state parks and trails dedicated to the moraines, drumlins, and coulees that remained after the ice receded. We're more interested in the large depressions those heavy glaciers carved into the ground, then filled with melted ice when the glaciers receded.

From the western Great Lakes to the Finger Lakes region of New York, the glaciers gouged out holes in the landscape. Even the hard granite of the Canadian Shield was no match for mile-thick ice, I'm told. We can thank the big blocks of ice for all those lakes that provide some of the continent's best fishing opportunities for cold-water species like walleyes, lake trout, and big northern pike. Fly over the waterworld of southern Canada, especially Ontario and Quebec, on a hunting or fishing trip, and the land looks like a creative afterthought—simple blobs of green amidst the blue lakescape.

Areas south of or between lobes of the glaciers created "driftless areas" where you won't find lakes. But the fact that glaciers didn't flatten this landscape means water has had time to erode the land and create hilly bluff country with cool meandering streams and rivers in between. Today many of those waterways contain excellent, underfished bassin' opportunities.

To this day, on my tournament circuit I'll still pursue smallmouth as far south as Arkansas, although many of my southern comrades admit

Opposite: Adult bass spend much of their life in ambush mode, waiting for unsuspecting food sources to stumble nearby and offer an easy meal. Bouncing a grub or artificial lure past or through shady structure can elicit strikes from largemouths on even the warmest, brightest days of the year.

that one reason they enjoy fishing northern tournaments is for the much greater opportunity to fish the hard-fighting, surface-busting smallmouth. Like largemouth, smallies have been stocked all over the place, but they demand cleaner, colder water than their greenish cousins.

Classic stocked smallmouth water includes much of the canoe country wilderness waterways of the Boundary Waters and Quetico region of northern Minnesota and northwest Ontario, the Adirondacks region of New York, and many points in between and elsewhere. But both species also are present in many lakes and riverways that you can access by boat, so let's break down where these fish are hiding.

Temperature-wise, largemouth are simply more tolerant of warmer water. The warmest water that ever produced largemouth for me was in the upper 80s, but most of my summertime, northern U.S. fish are in low 80-degree water. Down South they survive in waterways with summer temperatures into the high 80s. Unless it's in a large deepwater lake where they can find relief from warmer temps, most smallmouth I see prefer waterways that top out around 70 degrees. For that reason, you're rarely going to find a massive smallie in a farm pond or shallow, farm-country lake, and you're less likely to catch largemouth in a cold Canadian Shield lake. Like most American sportfish, both species require clean water, though the largemouth can survive or even thrive in less pristine waterways than the smallmouth. Given that those conditions persist across most of the Lower 48, it's no wonder that largemouth are the dominant bass species.

Even in these relatively warm lakes and reservoirs, largemouth bass seek cover for shade and to remain hidden prior to striking their prey. Vegetation, rocky outcroppings, docks, bridges, swimming platforms, or other structure offer obvious locations where you'll find bass. By the way, there's a fine line between too many weeds and not enough. A quality lake usually contains enough weeds for big bass to hide and hammer the small panfish. Too many weeds, however, prevent the bass from successfully preying on the sunnies, which can then destroy bass nests. It's a phenomenon we see on too many waterways and is one reason catch-and-release is so important. Release those big bass so they can chomp the sunnies and maintain healthier lakes. Exotic vegetation like curly-leaf pondweed and Eurasian water milfoil, which spread quickly and choke out balanced native vegetation, hasn't helped in this regard.

Because of their toughness and ability to survive in warmer water, you'll find largemouth in virtually every reservoir, river, stream, or marsh that's connected to any of our big river systems. (Walleyes inhabit many of the same waters.) Backwater areas of rivers or flooded timber provide excellent locations for finding largemouth bass. They've also been stocked just about anywhere else, including farm ponds dotted across much of America. But even though they're found in many places, we usually can locate bass in specific locations on any given waterway. It's not hard to decipher where these locations exist, so unlike other species of fish—say those oft-suspended, nomadic crappies—it's relatively easy to get efficient with your bass search.

It all boils down to one word: structure. This could mean many different things, including natural or man-made structure like flooded timber, sunken islands, riprap, or emergent vegetation like lily pads or bulrushes. In general, I've found that the more variety of habitats, the better the fishing.

Talkin' Largies

Largemouth long have been king in the southern United States, but even amateur anglers recognize that quality largemouth water exists north of the Mason-Dixon Line. The largemouth bass (*Micropterus salmoides*) grows larger than smallmouth bass and ranges much farther south—all the way into Mexico (where I've fished them) if you want to head way south. They grow larger than smallies in North Country, though not by much. The state record largemouth in my home state of Minnesota—8 pounds, 15 ounces—was caught in autumn 2005. Obviously that's a smidge smaller than George Perry's 22-pound, 4-ounce Georgia largemouth (which just marked its seventy-fifth anniversary in June 2007). The Gopher State's top smallmouth is 8 pounds, 0 ounce, so it's not much smaller than the Minnesota largemouth record. And it's not ridiculously smaller than the David Hayes world record 11-pound, 15-ounce Tennessee smallie caught in 1955.

Largemouth tend to run multiple shades of green in color and have a long, blotchy horizontal stripe running along their lateral line from gill plate to tail on both sides. I like this about largemouth—every fish looks unique and beautiful. Once you've caught enough largemouth and smallmouth bass, telling the difference between the two is ridiculously easy, but every new angler wants to understand the name difference—largemouth vs. smallmouth—so here goes. Looking at it from a profile view, the jaw of a largemouth bass is longer than on a smallmouth and stretches past the eye. On a smallie, the corner of the jaw ends rights below the eye. And, yes, when you lip-land a largemouth, its mouth does appear larger than your basic smallmouth—hence the nickname bigmouth, or bucketmouth.

Any tournament angler can tell you that in some parts of the country, largemouth grow faster and bigger thanks to a longer growing season. Even casual bassers know the largemouth record has nearly fallen a couple of times. California, with its huge warm-water reservoir fish, came close to creating a new world record in 2006 and is likely to produce the next record eventually. In my neck of the woods, most largemouth will weigh between 1 and 3 pounds, and I can find and fish bass of that size (9 to 19 inches) all day.

During winter, the warm water–loving largemouth loses it voracious appetite and becomes lethargic and much less aggressive. Spend some time reading outdoors pages and outdoors newspapers in the northern United States from February through April, and you won't see many headlines like "Top Lakes for Lunker Bass through the Ice," or "Seven Tips for Icing Bucketmouths." If bass aren't striking and fighting, we're usually not pursuing them. For that reason, largemouth bass fishing is a late-spring, summer, and early-autumn pursuit, and the hard-core anglers (yours truly) head south to warmer climes and open water to scratch that largemouth itch. (That's exactly how I caught my biggest bass ever, a double-digit specimen from Lake Amistad, Texas, in late October 2007. What a blast!) I believe many more bass these days survive a long time thanks to the growing catch-and-release ethic across the country.

Largemouth and smallmouth bass are predators; they'll eat just about any living, moving creatures they can catch: minnows, small-fry, or fingerlings, of virtually any species for breakfast; amphibians like frogs or salamanders for lunch; baitfish such as shad, small panfish or roughfish, and shiners for dinner; insects as appetizers; and crayfish for dessert. Land critters like shrews or mice and waterfowl such as ducklings in the water also are fair game for big bass. Like most creatures, however, bass prefer steady sources of forage, so they establish home territories near good feeding areas.

According to life history information on bass from the University of Minnesota, young bass eat mostly plankton and other tiny critters like waterfleas. They can put on weight fast, and in warmer southern climes they can become fishable their first year. We don't enjoy such speedy growth rates where I came of age as an angler, but during the shorter growing season in this part of the country, bass feed as actively and aggressively as anywhere else. As they grow, they move up the dining scale to the nymph stages of big insects like dragonflies, damselflies, and other bugs. Baitfish like small shad become the primary food source of adult bass, although worms, big insects, frogs, and crayfish end up in their bellies, too. Consequently, many fishing techniques we'll discuss in this book mimic these prey species.

As bass anglers, this affects how we fish, because we're trying to trick these predators into believing we're throwing food at them. Bass eat live food, and they seem to love the thrill of the chase more than other piscatorial species, which is one reason they're more fun to catch than, say, the not-so-humble walleye.

So as bass anglers we're mostly finding the natural food sources, then trying to match them via artificial offerings to garner more strikes. For example, the northern Mississippi River usually produces a good crop of baitfish every spring, so by midsummer you'd better believe I'm working flashy crankbaits at multiple depths in this waterway. In spring before much natural forage has bloomed, I'll work an artificial frog over lily pads or other matted vegetation. Rock areas, especially in clear water, with lots of nooks and crevices usually hold abundant crayfish, which largemouth and smallmouth bass alike absolutely love! There are a lot of plastics and crankbait lures that resemble crayfish—go figure!

Watching bass feed is amazing. I've seen underwater video and live bass in tanks up close, and largemouth will snap open their massive mouth and—in the blink of an eye—swallow whatever food source they're targeting. One second the baitfish is there; the next second that big old bucketmouth is sitting there with a contented look on his face. Big largemouth will consume big baitfish, which is a major reason you can use large lures when targeting largemouths. (Smallies, as a general rule, require a little more finesse.) I've seen 20-inch largemouth trying to swallow 6-inch baitfish—no kidding!

Largemouth bass target their prey a number of ways, but most largies that strike the end of my line usually are in ambush mode. They're hanging around some sort of shady structure—weeds, underwater branches or trees, or docks—and waiting for something tasty to swim past. This is especially true in late summer, when they're seeking relief from the sun and baitfish are in ample supply. Other times of year, particularly in spring, big largemouth are more likely to be patrolling the breakline or other, deeper structure for their next dinner.

Wherever I fish tournaments, when the water warms to about 60 to 65 degrees (in May and June in Minnesota), largemouth begin spawning in the shallows. Farther south, even into southern Illinois and Ohio, the bass spawn wraps up by late April most years. Multiple environmental factors trigger the spawn, and I've seen its timing vary by three weeks on a given lake from year to year. Male bass enter spawning areas to find prime nesting spots, then the females follow and drop thousands of eggs (according to professional fisheries reports, like the University of Minnesota's) in an area the male clears. He then guards the eggs, which hatch in a few days (depending on region), from panfish and other pesky predators.

Most states in the northern United States close the season for largemouth bass around the spawn to protect the fish from overzealous anglers. These fish are very susceptible to harvest during the spawn because they'll protect the nest at all costs. It may be great fun pulling that aggressive male off the nest with a flashy lure, but if the local panfish come gobble all the eggs while you're releasing him, you're hurting the next generation of bass and bass anglers! For that reason, I strongly urge all bass anglers, professional and amateur, North and South, to avoid fishing bass on the beds! When the young bass, called fry, hatch from the eggs, the male will hang around with them until they go their separate ways within a few days. It's tough out there for the fry—everything is trying to eat them—which is a major reason that mama bass produces so many eggs.

Just via simple visual observation, it's clear when the spawn is occurring on a given lake or reservoir. Once it starts, the spawn usually wraps up in a couple weeks in North Country because water can warm up through that prime spawning temperature range pretty fast. After the spawn, females especially can be difficult to catch because they're pretty hung over from the spawning process. Perhaps the females of any species can relate (I certainly can): We just want to be left alone! Within a couple of weeks, however, they're hungry again, and some of the best bass fishing of the year will commence.

A Basic Largemouth Search

The classic largemouth scenario probably breaks down like this: You're running your trolling motor from the front of your casting platform while casting into the weedy shallows that ring the shoreline. Behind you, the water gets deeper and the emergent, and eventually submergent, vegetation disappears. The shallow flats in front of you offer incredible foraging opportunities and spawning locations for early and late in the open-water season, but the deep water provides a more constant, temperate zone where bass, especially big bass, can find consistent temperatures during the extremes of the year—i.e., late summer and winter.

Find the "deep holes" where current, dredging, or the lake's natural formation has carved out a deep bottom, and you've probably found a prime zone for big fish seeking relief from extreme heat or cold. I won't call the deep flats "no fish land," but generally speaking, that's the last place I'll search for largemouth on lakes. Offshore structure could include a hump or emergent flats where bass may be holding on top or along the sides. As we'll discuss later, modern electronics, especially a GPS in tandem with some sort of contour mapping technology, can make researching such structure much easier.

When fishing the shallows, we're looking for specific types of areas that hold bass, and a common problem for anglers here is too much quality structure. Examples include submerged brush or other woody vegetation, points or small peninsulas that jut into the main lake basin (especially rocky points), or the slackwater areas with vegetation near some current. Moving water usually carries baitfish or other food sources, and largemouth love to be near such areas, ready to strike.

If I'm fishing a tournament on a reservoir situation—say, Lake Pepin on the Mississippi River—you're likely to find me working rocky riprap areas near culverts or just downstream of where a creek enters the lake. Too much good structure? This is one reason bass anglers have a reputation for moving a lot, because we're going to sample all of that good structure; if any one doesn't produce quickly, we're going to move on, fast! Look for areas that really stand out from surrounding lake contours or substrate, and try them first.

In between the shallows and the deep flats is the all-important breakline. This transition zone, which is almost like a mini-continental shelf (to make a saltwater analogy), marks the point where the shallow flats quickly drop off into deeper water. (Hint: When fishing a new lake, look for places on your contour map where the water gets deep fast.) Light disappears as the water deepens, so vegetation disappears, too. The breakline provides a corridor where bass will travel to other points of structure, as well as a safe area where bass may hold early and late in the day.

If casting the shallows is Bassin' 101 at the University of Fishing, then working a finesse worm off the breakline is Bassin' 201. Many seasoned bass anglers start at the breakline, especially early in the day before the shallows begin warming up. Watch for largemouth to congregate in the "inside turn" areas of a breakline where it forms a shallow bowl adjacent to a bay or corner of the shoreline. Combine an inside turn of a breakline with some simple structure, like green weeds early in the year, and you've got an absolute prime largemouth honey hole.

Classic deepwater locations for me usually mean finding some sort of submerged rocks or man-made structure (like fish cribs) that doesn't appear on any lake maps. These can run deeper than you might expect. I've pulled largemouth up from 15 or even 20 feet off a deep, rocky reef. Other places may be where some light current has slowly created an underwater edge that even the latest lake mapmaker hasn't located. Prime spots usually are near a sharp transition to a shallow area where big bass can feed, but then quickly retreat to the safety of deep water when fishing pressure or some other environmental factor drives them out of the shallows.

When I see such situations on a contour map, I'll use my depthfinder or my underwater video camera to scan it. Inevitably, there's something down there—a rock pile, an underwater hump, or a submerged bridge—where bass will stack up. Finding something like this is really exciting. I feel like a detective searching for clues, and when I find a spot like this, it makes my day! In a tournament situation, I'll always use my GPS to mark this structure and begin working around its edges. Any blips on the depthfinder that show unique structure along those edges usually represent what we bass loyalists call the "spot on a spot," and you'd better believe I'll fish that spot hard!

Farther north, on the edge of the largemouth's range, you'll sometimes encounter incredibly fast drop-offs just a few feet from the rocky shorelines of Canadian Shield–type waters. In case you haven't already noticed, bass love rocks, and even steep wall-like rocky structure will attract cruising bass. Southern bass gurus in Missouri and other locales know this rule, too. They'll often work the rocky limestone caves that jut underwater and provide that all-important shade for big, hungry bucketmouths.

Strictly Smallies

Smallmouth identification is easy after a little time on the water. When in doubt, check out the jaw. Note how its back corner ends below the eye. A largemouth's jaw extends to behind the eye.

Now let's talk strictly smallmouth *(Micropterus dolomieu)*, otherwise known as bronzebacks across most of their range. Bronzebacks have received that moniker thanks to their tanner, almost brownish color, and—though they can appear greenish, too—smallies always lack those distinctly dark horizontal markings along the lateral line that you see on a largemouth.

Quite the opposite, smallmouth have dark vertical bars that can appear every ½ inch or so along the fish's length. Their presence, or lack thereof, seems to vary from waterway to waterway. As I explained earlier, when in doubt, the back edge of the jaw stops right below the eye on a smallie; it does not extend beyond it as on a largemouth. Trust me, after you catch a few, bass ID is like cats and dogs.

That's despite the fact that smallmouth can show some remarkable color variation. Stress can change the color of almost any fish, and this rule truly applies to smallmouth. During the spawn on Lake Mille Lacs in central Minnesota, I've seen smallies look almost black. Keep any fish out of the water too long, and its brilliant colors will fade.

Generally you're going to find smallmouth in cooler, clearer water than the largemouth, although many lakes and rivers contain both species. They're found in the southern United States, too, but their range ends at much more northerly climes than the largemouth, extending deeper into Canada than Mr. Bucketmouth. In portions of the Upper Midwest, you'll find smallmouth in some of the same streams and rivers where you find brown trout. For that reason, smallmouth have become quite popular with the fly-angling set, and there's a nifty little subculture of anglers who use driftboats on big rivers or float-tube on small rivers while fly-casting for lunker smallmouth. Tie into a 3-pound smallie with a 5-weight fly rod and you're in for some exciting fishing!

Though they have a well-deserved reputation for preferring moving water, you'll find smallies in many northern lakes and reservoirs, especially with hard, sandy bottoms. To provide food and fishing sport, many smallmouth were stocked into cold border country lakes 100-plus years ago where they had never previously existed. For that reason, many visitors from places like Minnesota's Boundary Waters Canoe Area Wilderness have pictures of themselves hoisting up lunker, red-eyed smallmouth. A good rule of thumb: If you find robust smallmouth in a lake or river, you're probably fishing pretty healthy, clean water. I've caught them all across the central and eastern portions of the United States, including the Mississippi drainage, the St. Lawrence River, the Great Lakes, and a personal favorite smallmouth destination, New York/Vermont's Lake Champlain. (We'll talk more about those locations later.)

Smallmouth grow slower than largemouth, thanks partially to living in cooler, slower growing environments. But smallmouth simply don't grow as large as their bigmouth cousins, although you can catch many from 1 to 3 pounds across their range. Tennessee produced the world-record smallie, which weighed 11 pounds, 15 ounces and measured 27 inches long.

Because they're a cooler-water species, smallmouth demand more care with catch-and-release. I make sure my live well is very well oxygenated and as cool as possible before placing any fish into it, especially smallmouth. When practicing catch-and-release, please snap pictures quickly of your smallies, then quickly return them to the water. They're a hair more fragile than their bigmouth cousins, in my experience.

Predators like the largemouth, young smallmouth first consume plankton, then insects, working their way up to baitfish toward the end of their first summer. The classic smallmouth prey is crayfish, and I've caught many smallmouth over the years that are regurgitating these claw-snapping crustaceans. Perhaps it's because in a colder environment, smallmouth must be more versatile in targeting prey species, but even more so than largemouth bass, smallmouth love smacking topwater lures, a technique we'll describe more later. Because they live in more northerly locations, they spawn later than largies and in slightly cooler water—often getting motivated with nest building when water temperatures are in the high 50s.

Do I prefer smallmouth to largemouth or vice versa? I love them both; though, if forced to choose, I'd definitely say smallmouth, simply because they're symbolic of the wonderful cool lakes, rivers, and streams in the portion of the country where I grew up. There's just something about these feisty little brown bass that is utterly addictive. Outside the trout and salmon family, they probably fight harder pound for pound than any other freshwater fish. One second a large smallmouth is burrowing your lure into the sediment under the boat, and the next he's breaking water and sizzling line off your reel. In my part of the country, many anglers can recount their first success story with a big smallmouth; the species inspires young and old alike.

Here's a little secret about smallmouth that most tournament folks would never give away: Smallies are curious little buggers that notice anything out of place. That's why simple techniques like deadsticking (i.e., leaving a lure lying on the bottom or topwater, then maybe just twitching it occasionally) drive smallmouth nuts. Leave a lure in their neighborhood long enough, and they just can't resist!

Smallmouth Locations

Smallmouth locations are very much like largemouth locations, although they demand higher water quality, which eliminates them from a good chunk of the largemouth's range. They prefer a harder bottom than largemouth, and they're willing to stay in deeper water longer than their larger cousins to find the bottom structure and safety zone they demand. Smallies love rocks even more than largemouth bass, especially large boulders that cast some shade. Some of the best football-size smallmouth locations on Lake Mille Lacs in central Minnesota feature just a few big rocks or small boulders in 7 or 8 feet of water.

Where you have rocks and clear, cool water, you probably have crayfish. These mini-"lobsters" provide a nutritious food source for bass (particularity smallies), which consider them culinary delights. Try working such areas with crankbaits that mimic crayfish.

To summarize, smallmouth are more finicky, and smart bass anglers use this trait to their advantage. You need four key elements for smallmouth: a clean environment, shade, forage, and the availability of both deep- and shallow-water habitats. Find that spot, say a rocky bar or clump of vegetation, that contains smallmouth, and mark it in your GPS. Odds are that many lunker-smallmouth anglers know the spot. (This is also a reason smallmouth catch-and-release is so important! Once anglers locate these places, it's all too easy to really hammer these slow-growing fish.)

Even in weedy areas, smallmouth want to stay over a hard bottom. Mucky-bottom areas on warmer, what seasoned anglers and biologists call "eutrophic," lakes (where algae blooms occur or nonnative exotics like milfoil thrive) rarely contain smallmouth bass. It's those low-nutrient, coldwater, "oligotrophic" lakes with long sandy or rocky bottoms areas that we want to work for smallmouth. Find me a big old white pine toppled over a hard-sloping, gravelling bottom over a clear-water lake, and I'll catch you a smallmouth bass, every time!

Earlier, I mentioned finding steep rocky outcroppings in Canadian Shield waters for the northernmost largemouth bass. Well, if you're too far north for largies, I can almost guarantee you'll pull a big smallmouth from a rocky gap or underwater ledge. If I can leave the novice angler with one simple rule for smallies, it's this: Find the rocks!

CHAPTER TWO

Influences on Success

The Mother Nature Factor

Once you succeed (or think you've succeeded) in understanding basic bass fishing locations, Mother Nature throws you a wicked curve ball. We can summarize that nasty pitch in one word: weather. Everything I just explained about bass haunts and locations depends on a fairly stable weather pattern. That translates into consistent temperatures and clear skies or a few high clouds. Seems like most of this decade, for whatever reason, the only thing constant about the weather is change. I rarely plan a tournament around a stable weather pattern, and the first thing I check before heading to an event is the weather report. Like I said, I expect something, but the severity and type of weather can change my plans and determine what locations I'll work on a given body of water.

Bass become significantly less predictable before, during, and after a weather front. The change in air pressure, temperature, and disturbance to the water column from additional direct rain, wind, or runoff all can affect the position and mood of the fish. Think about it: Their entire environment has changed—they can't go indoors like you or I—so it's no surprise that they act a little weird. In my experience, bass of all sorts throw on the feedbag prior to a front's arrival, but no two words frustrate tournament anglers more than "cold front." There's not a tournament angler alive who hasn't enjoyed excellent prefishing before an event, only to have an early summer cold front shut down the bite.

Animals can sense impending weather changes better than humans, and prior to a storm is a great time to be on the water chucking something aggressive. Usually, however, Murphy's Law demands that day one of a tournament opens about six hours after a front arrives, when the bass aren't feeding or active. Later we'll talk about a finesse approach, and here's one time that demands it.

The most common weather factor that will challenge almost any angler is wind, and let me be frank here: I hate wind! Novice (and not-so-novice) fly-anglers and spinning-reel users alike struggle with casting and proper lure placement in windy conditions. Casting into a breeze is an exercise in frustration, so whenever possible, position yourself or your boat so you're casting with the wind. (You'll be amazed how much farther you can cast!) Boat control also becomes more difficult, so mastering your trolling-motor technique will help in properly positioning your watercraft. In really high winds, the resulting rough water can become hazardous, and on big lakes (or even small lakes) I simply won't fish if the overall weather conditions become too dangerous. No event, or fish, is worth risking my life.

Wind also can alter the behavior and location of the fish, but we can use that fact to our advantage. A windblown shoreline almost works like a stream, river, or any other place with current. Tip: With any type of fishing, water with some turbulence (think "stirring") contains food that attracts big fish like bass. Walleye guys know this tip well, too, and in the right conditions this can produce phenomenal fishing. We'll get into specific lures and tactics later, but these windblown shorelines are good places to toss spinnerbaits or—if you know the water is deep enough—even crankbaits.

Rain (and sometimes snow at my really early-season tournament events) often accompanies wind. Downpours aren't fun to fish under, but in my experience light rain or stalled-out gray skies usually help the fishing. Spend enough time outdoors and you'll appreciate recreating under clouds rather than a beating-hot sun. When wind or heavy rain gets so severe that you begin to feel unsafe on the water, tell yourself this: You're probably not missing prime fishing. The fish feel the same way about the turbid, unstable water conditions and have bailed out of the shallows. In my experience, they're off to spend two or three days in a deepwater funk.

Here's a windy silver lining: While avoiding wind in my prime locations, I've discovered some great new fishing spots that I otherwise never would have found. Even on tough weather days, you probably can find a hidden bay or inlet sheltered enough to safely drop a line. Over time, you'll develop windy-day options, and these same spots—which you probably ignored before—might become prime water even under clear skies.

Boating Equipment

Bass are a popular species to fish for many reasons, but one is that—thanks to the sheer luck of evolution—they're found virtually everywhere in the country. They're aggressive, hungry, and love the shallows, so citizens of all backgrounds and income levels can enjoy catching this fish. Part of the beauty of catching bucketmouths is that you don't need a boat. Millions of people in this country enjoy fishing bass from shore, from float tubes, or from other small watercraft not considered classic "bass boats." Back when my children were smaller, my husband and I would take them to Cedar Lake outside Annandale, Minnesota. I'd spend hours on a windsurfing board (minus the sail) kicking around the breakline fishing bass. Our family dog at the time would sun himself on the bow, providing a nice balancing counterweight while I fished.

Though I firmly believe you can fish bass from shore all day, sometimes chasing this species means working big water. Perhaps you'll develop into a serious bass angler and consider the tournament scene. Whatever the reason, many recreational anglers often ask me about my boat, so in this section I want to describe what qualifies as the perfect bass rig for Karen Savik.

If you've got a fat checkbook, you can spend as much as you want on a bass boat. Some folks go overboard spending-wise, but there are basic features that make a boat more practical for this style of fishing. On small water, virtually any shallow-hulled craft will suffice. One of my friends who grew up along the Upper Mississippi River fished his entire youth making short multispecies trips on a flat-bottom aluminum duck-hunting boat.

The first time he fished in my fiberglass V-hull, he sat amazed. "Wow, I didn't know you could ride over waves like this and not feel your spine being crushed," he said. Yeah, any boat will do, but if you're going to spend serious weeks every summer targeting bass, invest in a more comfortable experience.

I fish a 20-foot fiberglass, shallow V-hull with a 96-inch (8-foot) beam powered by a 225-horse Evinrude E-Tech. Here's why that works for me. Glass boats run a little quieter than aluminum rigs, though you're going to spend more for fiberglass. They're heavier, but again, I like the smoothness and the variability in fiberglass hulls, in terms of design and length. Why the V-hull? Well, unlike my friend's flat-bottom, which—to its credit—went anywhere in those Mississippi River backwaters via a Go-Devil motor on the stern, a V-hull cuts through the waves and delivers a much smoother ride. That's important for a tournament angler like me who covers miles of water every day, though even rank-and-file fishermen and women will appreciate the comfort. That said, the key word in "shallow V-hull" is "shallow." You still want to access those weedy bays and lily pads where a deep-V walleye rig would bottom out. Hence the shallow-draft bass boat: the best of both worlds!

Bass anglers are casters. We like clearance, serious boat control, and an unencumbered view—i.e., low gunwales and an open casting platform. Standing around, talking, and casting on a bluebird day is a key reason I love bass fishing so much, and I suspect there are a lot of people just like me. The classic bass boat has evolved from these demands. Wind can't push the low-profile hull of a bass boat around as much as a deeper V-hull walleye rig, and those low gunwales mean a clearer view (and shot) for casting. As for that wide, 8-foot beam, it's a tight fit in the garage, but I like the space for gear storage compartments and my casting platform. Narrower bows may look big enough, but put yourself up there with a trolling motor, a depthfinder, and a tackle box, and you'll catch yourself tripping over gear. Even at that width, I'll catch myself thumping into my bump seat up front. Make sure you can move that (incredibly handy) bump seat when you don't feel like sitting or leaning against it.

As a tournament angler, this girl hits some big water, and I simply feel more comfortable in a 20-foot boat running over big waves than in an 18-footer or smaller. Wind can change in an instant, and when rough weather rolls in, that 225-horse motors me back to shore fast. Though you're more

Opposite: I fish a 20-foot fiberglass, shallow V-hull with a 96-inch beam powered by a 225-horsepower Evinrude E-Tech.

likely to encounter potentially dangerous water on the Great Lakes, which I fish several times per year, it can happen on smaller lakes or rivers, too.

Lake Mille Lacs in central Minnesota, for example, has excellent smallmouth fishing. Many, many anglers in the Gopher State can share some frightening stories about "big rollers" on this 13-mile-wide lake. And don't believe anyone who says you can't fish docks in a 20-foot boat; I do it all the time. If you're fishing small, 1,500-acre lakes and reservoirs and never anticipate fishing serious big water, a 14- or 16-footer will suffice. Avoid going much smaller than that. Here's why.

Bass anglers like stuff. We own multiple tackle boxes, dozens of rods, all-weather gear for any circumstance, electronics many people can't even pronounce, and accessories galore! You're going to want a boat with storage containers, plus that wide casting platform. You'll want a live well, preferably an insulated one to keep fish cool on hot days, with an

When bass fishing becomes an addiction, like it has for me, you will find yourself in desperate need of storage space for all the lures and other "essential" gear you have purchased. When you take the plunge and buy yourself a serious bass boat, make sure it has ample storage for all your tackle.

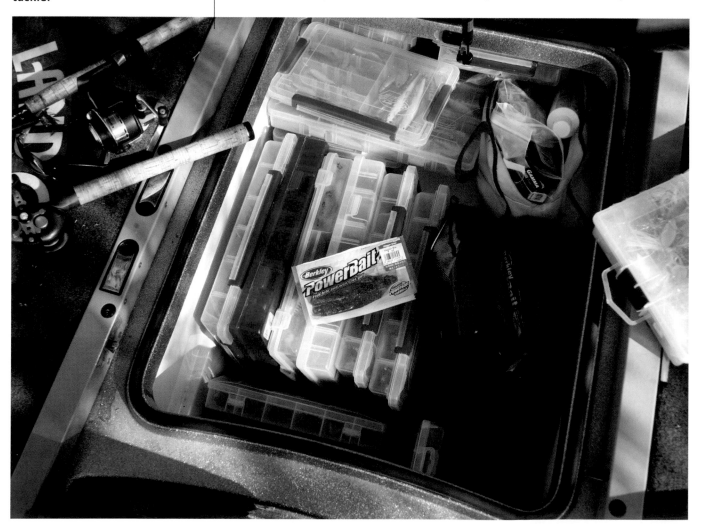

aerator. (Even when I intend to release a fish, I throw it in the live well to reinvigorate it in the oxygen-rich water for a little while.)

Other mandatory equipment includes a bow-mounted trolling motor and a couple of depthfinders—one in the console and one by my trolling motor. An automatic bilge pump keeps water out of your craft, and an onboard charger attaches to your batteries and ensures that they're charging when you plug it in at night. Every boat should be properly outfitted with lights, mostly to help other boats avoid you. I fish bass frequently at dusk, so I'm constantly checking and monitoring my lights. My ideal boat also has a lot of rod locker storage (to hold at least twelve rods), plus other spare compartments for a lot of gear. I like it manageable, not plumb full. Most people these days rely on cell phones and Blackberries for monitoring weather more than all-weather radios, but it's still a good idea to have a quality radio running, especially on big water.

By the way, the water pressure gauge is the most important dial on that console. Boat manufacturers put a massive rock-and-roll speedometer on the console (which rarely works), then an itty-bitty water pressure gauge. Personally, I'm way more interested in whether my motor is getting enough water to cool it than whether I can run faster than the next guy. (I usually

It is important to have two aerated live wells that keep the fish alive and happy. It also provides plenty of room for that great catch.

can monitor my speed via the RPM or GPS reading anyway.) This angler is not a "need for speed" kind of gal, but I like that big horsepower when it's necessary. As a tournament angler, you never know when you'll need to head in quick for a weigh-in or to avoid nasty weather.

I'm also hearing more questions on multibladed props. I still prefer a three-blade prop because it gives me more top-end speed when I'm covering water. You lose a couple miles per hour with four- and five-blade props, but they give you that initial burst of speed that some tournament guys prefer at shotgun-start events, or for taking off in shallow water.

As for trailers, a couple of quick thoughts: Backing up is easier with a single-axle trailer, but bigger boats, like my own, require a tandem axle. Bottom line: Make sure when you buy a boat that you have plenty of motor and trailer to support it. I will add that trailers with steps are great; that's a fabulous idea that should have been thought of long ago!

Fishing Electronics

Although bass anglers don't rely on electronics as much as the average walleye angler, they're still very important. But electronics intimidate beginning anglers for a couple of reasons. First, if you're unfamiliar with them, they look pretty complicated. Second, you can spend a lot of money on them. Let's dispel those notions quickly. The average angler can buy simple electronics that encompass 90-plus percent of the top-of-the-line models' basic functions at an affordable price, and you can learn to use them quickly. Yes, you catch fish without electronics, but you'll become more efficient, and frankly have more fun, with a couple of these devices in your bass-fishing tool kit.

The depthfinder is the one piece of fishing electronics I absolutely would not fish without. There are many styles and price ranges, but bottom line, this device tells you (at least) the depth of the water you're fishing. A depthfinder reveals the humps and structure underneath your boat to provide a clear view of the bottom content, and this information correlates directly to which type of presentation you should employ. Want a clear view of the breakline or structure that could hold bass? A quality depthfinder can unveil every nook and cranny. Via a transducer, depthfinders relay a good old-fashioned sonar signal off the bottom to provide an accurate

Today's liquid-crystal graphs combine depthfinder technology with GPS and lake map data to create an absolutely indispensable unit for any angler. Prices have dropped to the point that just about anyone can justify the expense.

depth reading. Simple round dial–style flashers run a little cheaper and offer some insight into whether large fish or baitfish are present. They don't, however, provide a history of what happened 5 yards back, so if you're distracted when you pass over a large fish, a flasher won't tell you what you missed. I keep one in my boat, however, because they seem to provide more accurate depth readings when I'm scouting at higher speeds. I also believe they show more consistent readings through thick weeds.

What you need is a liquid crystal display graph, which shows you an actual picture on a miniscreen of the water your boat has passed over, including crisp Vs or delineations showing fish. Anglers new to LCD graphs often misinterpret what they're seeing, but with experience, you'll be amazed at the detail and specific underwater information one of these devices can provide. For monitoring bottom structure, you can't beat a multidimensional picture, and that's just what an LCD graph illustrates. High-resolution, color-display graphs have been dropping in price in recent years and have become the standard on the LCD market. Most mark fish at ridiculously deep depths, way beyond the needs of most bass anglers. If you get seriously into fishing, you'll want both a flasher and an LCD, and these days you really don't even need to choose. There are many combo units on the market with split screens, with a flasher bar on one side of the LCD screen, or you can switch between the two with a flick of a button. If you want to spend even more, there are many units that combine sonar and GPS, which I'll talk about shortly.

When you buy a unit, consider the cone angle of the transducer—the device that concentrates that sonar sound into a beam. Imagine a cone with the tip starting at the transducer, then widening as the water deepens, and you'll better understand this concept. It's the area the sonar wave covers. A transducer with a narrower cone angle concentrates the signal, which translates into better resolution on the screen. The better the resolution, the better information you have on what's swimming below—maybe a lunker hawg. The trade-off with great resolution is that you see a narrower area and miss marking potentially big fish nearby. That's why LCD manufacturers sell multibeam transducers: one (or more) for a wide view and one for a narrow, higher res view. One practical rule of thumb to remember here is that the shallower the water, the smaller the cone angle. Finally, these units really have dropped in price since I started fishing. A quick Web search revealed fine black-and-white models for a couple hundred dollars. You can even buy little hand-held models for backcountry fishing.

When you begin getting serious about bass fishing from a boat, invest in a good depthfinder. Obviously, multitransducer models cost more, and the sky is the limit on features and gadgets with high-end models. I don't use half the bells and whistles on my depthfinder, but any unit in my boat will have a water temperature gauge, and I make sure its gain (sensitivity) is easily adjustable. Bottom line: A depthfinder will take your fishing to the next level—you'll see and investigate more structure that you wouldn't know existed without it. You can get better deals on closeout model "fish finders" during late summer or fall, and a sport show is a great place to see dozens, or even hundreds, of units in one place and get some hands-on learning with one.

New and improved depthfinders hit the market every year with all sort of added gadgets and features, even though its basic function as a sonar unit hasn't changed much. Another facet on the electronics scene has changed dramatically for the better the past ten or twelve years, though—Global

Positioning System (GPS) units. These devices triangulate information from the U.S. government's satellite systems to tell you your exact position to the nearest few feet, and they've improved tremendously in accuracy and reliability since I began using them fifteen years ago. You can buy battery-powered handheld or mounted, large-screen LCD graphlike models, even units that incorporate other features, like depthfinders.

GPS serves two primary navigation features: For starters, although it's less of a concern if you're fishing a small lake or pond down the road, GPS has an important safety role when fishing big water. Many big-water boaters and anglers around the world rely on GPS to help navigate them home (and through safe water) when low-visibility weather arrives. I wouldn't participate in a Great Lakes or any other big-water tournament event without my GPS. To be frank, even on calm days, GPS has helped lead me through some confusing stretches of water. (I once fished an event south of New Orleans that had a dizzying number of inlets, islands, side channels, and peninsulas that all looked the same to me. I'd still be slowly wandering through those bayous if it weren't for my GPS!) Handheld units are handy because you can use them for hiking or other non-boat-related activities, but I love my mounted model with its wide, easy-to-read screen and steady power supply from my boat's batteries.

As for fishing, you can plug specific waypoint coordinates into a GPS unit so that you can return to that same spot again and again. If you're willing to spend more money, you can buy units that incorporate maps of specific lakes, complete with structure and depth contours. Many tournament anglers plot likely points to investigate on an upcoming event on their home computer, then upload them to their GPS before even leaving home. The dominant trend in fishing electronics today is combining features within one unit.

The underwater camera hit the fishing scene like a whirlwind in the late 1990s, and many anglers use them for year-round fishing. A cable connects the underwater camera to the main unit and a small viewing screen in the boat. I keep one in my boat for those times when I want to get a direct look at the bottom content, structure, or even a fish that's frustrating me by refusing to bite. You're not going to get a plasma TV–like picture of anything, but you can't argue with the proof of actual sight and direct video. That said, buy a depthfinder and GPS unit first when you take your wallet to the fishing electronics section of your favorite sporting goods store.

CHAPTER THREE

Hitting the Water

Casting Tips

OK, let's start thinking about getting our line in the water. Casting is more than effectively dropping a lure into the sweet spot. Different styles of casting and—more importantly—retrieves create different angles that can present the same lure in very different ways. More than once while fishing, I've thrown a lure with nary a sniff, then cast so that it lands and runs at a different angle—and watched in amused disbelief as a big bass swallows it whole.

To cast successfully, your equipment—rod, reel, line, and lure—must be properly balanced. The occasional angler need not become too hung up on this, but to truly maximize the potential of the many often subtle techniques described in these pages, you need control over your cast. And that usually means balanced equipment. It starts with the lure, and the rule of thumb is: The heavier the lure, the stouter the rod. That's one reason tournament anglers own so many rods.

Sure, they could cast huge lures on ultralight equipment, and vice versa, but for precise casts, this tournament girl tries to match rod and lure as perfectly as possible. Don't worry; you don't need two dozen rods rigged with every style of lure in every action. Tournament folks operate that way because rerigging during fishing time can cost them fish. The average bass enthusiast can cover all his or her bases with three or four rods ranging in length from 6 feet to a 7-footer in increasing actions. We'll discuss which rod when in the presentation section.

As for casting, when you're looking for serious distance and the prospect of a louder splash doesn't bother you, go with the basic but powerful overhand cast, which maximizes the loading power of a given rod. If there's a piece of structure that I can cast past safely, I have no problem with the fast-and-dirty overhand cast. Bring the handle to about a twelve o'clock position, allow the rod a second to load behind you, then bring your hand quickly forward to a ten o'clock position. After the lure splashes down, I'll usually let it sit until the ripples dissipate, then begin my retrieve to alleviate the initial shock of the splash.

With a sidearm cast, you lose some of your rod's loading power, but it allows you to reach those spots where the overhand cast has no chance. "Skipping docks," where we're literally sneaking the lure under a horizontal structure, is a classic example. Get your body as low as possible, then, in simple terms, make a light overhand cast with your arm at 90 degrees (perpendicular) to your body. It's super-easy; the hardest part is control—

I use these great Fenwick rods and reels for ten to twelve hours a day, five to seven days per week. Make sure they are light and sensitive.

not tossing it with too much force. Finesse people, finesse! Another well-known "skipping" cast technique involves a quick wrist flick rather than a full-armed casting motion.

Flipping and pitching are subtle but more technical casting techniques that lend themselves best to jigs or Texas-rigged plastics. Your goal: to quietly enter holes, heavy cover, or turbid water to find lethargic bass. Flipping has become especially popular, or at least necessary, in lakes heavily infested with milfoil. Huge, thick mats of this exotic plant hold bass, which especially seem to appreciate its shade during late summer's heat, but it's next to impossible to retrieve anything through the thick stuff. Flipping evolved among savvy bassers, and it's a simple concept.

Quietly take your boat into the milfoil areas, and watch for holes or spaces in the vegetation combined with some sort of structure. There should be a lot of them, and they're typically where bass await their next meal, especially in midsummer, when the milfoil is lush and really growing. With your boat perched 12 to 15 feet away, let out anywhere from 12 to 18 feet of line, then grab the line (closed bail) by your rod's first line guide and pull as much back as possible. Then simply swing your lure close to surface toward the hole you want to fish, releasing the line in your hand as you do so. This takes a little practice (it's all in the wrist!) to become pinpoint accurate, but overall it's a simple, quiet technique.

In my experience, bass will often grab your jig-and-pig or rig on the drop or just as your begin your retrieve, so be ready to take up your slack quickly. If nothing strikes, try bouncing it a few times before retrieving it. Flipping doesn't excite most bass anglers as much as the image of big largemouth nailing a burning spinnerbait, but it's effective, and many tournament anglers have won events because flipping the foil worked when nothing else performed. The basic casting motion of flipping also works well with some surface lures, like artificial frogs or silver minnows that you'll drag over lilies or matted weeds.

Pitching is an actual open-bail cast, with more of a shooting motion that allows you to fire the lure under docks or low-hanging branches. And though it's more complicated than flipping, you can target farther spots. Release enough line so that your free hand can hold your lure about even with the reel. Place a little tension on the line, then, while moving the rod tip toward the hot spot, release the lure from your hand. The combination of tension and sweep from your rod provides the lure's forward momentum.

Get good with this technique, and you can quietly drop a lure into a choice location up to 30 feet out.

Since you're often retrieving lures farther, pitching usually works better in water with less dense vegetation. Both methods perform anywhere, anytime that stealth is a driving factor—say during night fishing—and even in clear water. My flippin' and pitchin' tactics increase later into midsummer, when largemouth and smallmouth alike already have seen the greatest hits of bass lures and are becoming increasingly skittish. Both require a medium-heavy, 7-foot-plus rod and heavy braided line to pull fish out quickly after the hookset.

With all your casting, don't be afraid to practice on the water, or even in the backyard. Pull the trebles off an old crankbait or rig a plastic sans hooks, then mess around on the lawn with some old line. Our time on the water is precious, so a little practice over the green grass of spring is time well spent. Just replace your line when you're done; any nicks or excessive dirt (which will foul your reel) can cost you a fish later.

Bass Presentations

Let me step out on a limb here and make a bold statement: No species of fish demands that anglers become more versatile with their techniques as black bass. Think about it! With muskies, you're mostly trolling or casting. Walleyes are a jigging, live-bait rigging, or crankbait special—either trolling or casting. Panfish, though many magazine articles and purists are diversifying, remain a jig, hook, and/or live-bait program. OK, now consider bass. There's finesse rigging, pitching and flipping, crankbaiting and spinnerbaiting, topwater, jig-and-pigging, spooning, drop-shotting … hell, virtually any technique that other freshwater anglers employ for their species of choice, you can use for fishing bass!

So many factors can determine which bass fishing presentation to use at any given time. Weather, time of year, the type of water, depth, and clarity: It's almost mind-boggling, even from someone who has fished tournaments for nearly fifteen years. Looking back at these past few sentences, I think I've ably summarized why bass fishing is so much fun. Later we'll talk about how to tackle those intangible factors we all encounter while bass fishing.

So without further ado, how about we tear into the meat and potatoes of bass fishing and talk tactics. I'll start with the basics: classic plastic worm rigging.

Plastics Rigging

OK, let's talk rubber worms or, more accurately in today's world, the plastic worm—or, in old-school talk, the rubber worm. They're not much to look at—although they do come in thousands of pretty colors and shapes—but no lure/presentation is more important in bass fishing than the plastic worm. They're relatively cheap, can be rigged multiple ways, and generations of bass have just loved their lifelike movement and natural-feeling, pliable bodies.

Let's get some terminology straight here first: A number of lures fall into the category of plastics, including grubs and tubes. A worm looks pretty much like a real nightcrawler with color variations. When you hear a bass angler refer to a "grub," she means the curly-tailed-style plastic like a Mr. Twister. A tube jig has a thick, bullet-nosed, hollow body with a bunch of squiggly legs dangling off the back. They're available in multiple sizes, depending on the aggressiveness of the fish, and with the new scented offerings from companies likely Berkley, fish like the way plastics smell, too. And unlike a crawler, which will squirm off your hook and provide at most a one-hit presentation, you can often fish the same plastic worm, grub, or tube for hours. Fishing a wilderness lake where bass, smallies especially, have never encountered a scented plastic worm is almost unfair—it's that effective. Plastic "worm" is probably too narrow a definition, because they come in many sizes and shapes: salamander, crayfish, leeches, frogs, and whatever else lure manufacturers' imaginations can conjure up.

A great trait about plastics is that bass don't become conditioned to these lures as quickly as most other hardbaits. On some urban, heavily fished metro lakes, I know anglers that use virtually nothing but a finesse worm for that very reason. They're also arguably the most versatile presentation available to bass anglers; they can be fished in weeds, off docks, or "swum" anywhere in the water column.

Because they tend to lose their action in colder water, plastic rigs remain first a warm-water presentation, though that's not to say they're ineffective in cold or cooling water. Unlike a spinnerbait or crankbait that sends a pulse through the water to the fish's lateral line, bass attack a plastic worm

Opposite: Every effective bass angler in America can probably hoist a handful of plastic worms, grubs, and tubes. Bass seem to become conditioned to hard baits, especially by late summer. Properly rigged finesse worms produce bass in all seasons in every region of the country.

simply because they see its forage-imitating action and want to consume it. Therefore, plastics rigging will perform best in clear or stained water (where bass can see it), not turbid farm ponds.

The basic plastic worm rig employs an offset long-shanked hook, pressed in through the top of the plastic, then flipped with the point of the hook ever so slightly reinserted into the meaty portion of the worm. This creates the "ah-ha" moment with a plastic worm: It's now weedless. (OK, pretty weedless.) You can cast it out and jig it back through light weeds, or virtually anywhere else, without getting hung up. Of course it's never quite that simple, but with practice you'll be amazed at how you're able to avoid picking up weeds with this presentation.

Add a ³⁄₁₆- to ³⁄₈-ounce bullet-headed sinker (you can modify it with a toothpick jammed between the sinker hole and line if you want to prevent it from moving; useful in some situations), and you've got what's known as a Texas rig. Don't ask me why it's called that. If it's a screw-in sinker, we bassin' folks call it a Florida rig. Move the weight up with a 15- to 30-inch leader between it and the plastic, and it's called a Carolina rig. The former (Texas) performs better in heavier cover, since that weight is near the plastic. In light cover such as shallow, grassy weeds, Carolina rigs perform well thanks to that added bit of movement. Another important function of the Carolina rig is to allow the angler to present the bait at a controlled distance above the lake bottom. In the same situation, you can also employ a basic jighead.

Place a glass bead between your hook and sinker, and you've got what bass pros call a doodle rig. The clicking and clacking of the glass bead helps generate reaction strikes from lethargic fish. Because you're looking to irritate the fish, a long slow retrieve—just inch that baby along—helps to prompt strikes. Technical tip: Learn to be a line watcher. Watch your line all the time, and you'll begin to recognize the subtle differences of how the line reacts to the bottom, to snags, and, most importantly, to fish. This rule applies more to plastics rigging that any other style of bass fishing. Wearing sensitive gloves and putting a finger on your line helps in this regard, too.

Start with larger 7- to 10-inch worms (with a 3/0 or 4/0 hook) when fishing largemouths and smaller 5- to 7-inch worms (and smaller hooks) for smallies. When you see or hear the term "finesse worm," we're talking about smaller, typically darker colored plastic rigs that finicky,

less-aggressive fish are willing to pursue. In high-pressured areas I work smaller finesse worms a lot. As for line, when rigging plastics I usually stick to fairly lightweight monofilament, from six- to twelve-pound test, on a pretty stiff baitcasting rod. You'll need a strong rod for those times when lures or fish bury themselves in the weeds, and it also helps set the hook through the plastic and into the fish.

Another prime plastic finesse approach for targeting finicky bass via spinning tackle is drop-shotting. The twist with drop-shotting is that it creates a more vertical presentation via a small hook and finesse plastic worm positioned 8 to 12 inches above a small, special ¼- to ½-ounce weight. With the weight holding the setup vertical, you can almost walk the presentation back to the boat with a semitaut line, and the plastic remains up off the bottom. Many bass anglers focus this technique in areas around steep structure like riprap or bridge pilings, and although that's an obvious place, I'll work drop-shots off breaklines, just to mix things up during a tough bite.

Add a leader and swivel, then move the weight in front of the swivel, and you've got yourself a Carolina rig. The space between the lure and the leader adds some action, making it a good lure to use in rocks and light weeds.

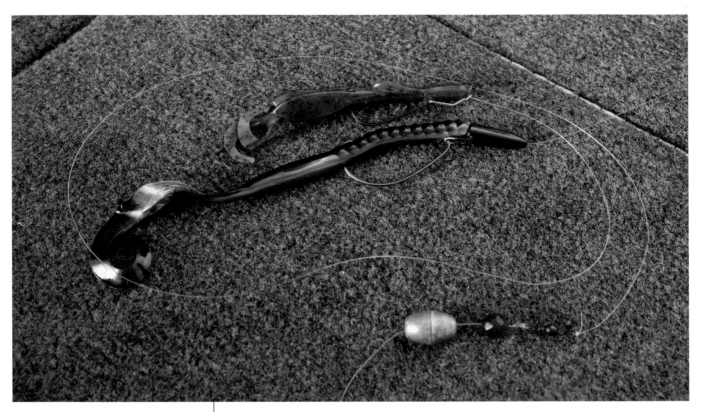

Remarkably enticing and pretty darn weedless, Texas and Carolina rigs remain among the most popular bass-fishing setups of all time.

Another option is to consider fishing your plastics rig weightless. Once, while suffering through a long, unproductive tournament day, my partner and I could see suspended fish slowly cruising around the boat, but our Texas rigs kept spooking them, despite our small (⅛-ounce) weights. Fed up and with nothing to lose, I cut off the sinker and threw the rig weightless. It worked. Within minutes, we found ourselves catching fish and back in the competition. The weightless option has been a productive part of my arsenal ever since.

When working your worm, you'll mostly want to use a classic lift-drop jigging motion. Cast it out to the edge of a weed flat, leaving enough line for it to drop—but not too much, or you'll miss the strike. Then begin pulling your rod tip to 90 degrees before letting your lure slowly drop again while taking up slack line. Repeat the process as you bring your lure back toward the boat, and monitor your line closely as that lure drops back down. (Be a line watcher!) One location hint here: Inside weed lines see significantly less pressure than outside weed lines. The water typically runs shallower, but with a little stealth you'll get some hookups.

Plastics rigging scares some people because it takes a fair amount of time on the water, mostly via trial and error, to develop the deft touch sometimes necessary to detect strikes. Hang in there, because once you figure it out, plastic worm rigging is great fun—and incredibly effective. Ask any bass angler what tool he or she couldn't live without while fishing, and you'd probably hear "plastics."

As I explained earlier, bass will lightly envelope a lure, so you may not notice a hard-core strike. Any line movement sideways, as well as a telltale, serious thump, probably signals a hit. Take up your slack line, then set the hook by swiftly pulling that rod tip back to 90 degrees. As with any fish at this point, keep your line tight and rod tip skyward. You're having fun now, but keep that fish under your control and moving toward you. Bass often live in thick cover, and you don't want that lunker to wrap itself around vegetation and get itself loose. Sometimes, especially in classic smallie water, I'll just tease bass by letting my rig play dead, then maybe I'll flick my wrist and scoot it forward a smidge. It drives those curious smallies nuts, and if I can be patient with this presentation, it produces fish!

Manufacturers sell most soft plastics in zip-lock-style bags. Store them there so that they remain pliable and don't dry out. Replace in an airtight bag properly (keeping colors separated), and you can get several uses out of a plastic worm. Though some of the newer plastic-style lures are biodegradable, many brands still are not. After several bass have pounded the life out of one, please dispose of it properly. Never throw line in the water, where it could sit for decades or choke something, like a loon.

Stickworms

Every bass tournament angler in North America keeps some fat-looking worms in their tackle box these days. The Senko-style worm looks like a long (usually 5 to 8 inches) slug, or a droopy magic marker, and the wacky rig that's evolved for their use has won a lot of tournaments this decade. Also called soft stickbaits, plastics like the Slug-Go and Fluke have a thick head and usually a narrower tail portion with an overall shapeless profile. They're not much to look at, but in the hands of a competent stick, they'll provide some enticing action because they mimic baitfish. When the chips are down, many tournament anglers turn to the soft stickbait—sometimes called a stickworm.

Hooked through the middle via a 5/0 hook, they flutter slowly to the bottom in what's called a wacky rig. (I mean literally "through the middle" so that the ends of the plastic dangle off both sides of the hook.) This technique, as I'll explain more later, has worked well for me with postspawn bass, when they often remain in a defensive, protect-the-beds mode. Taunt them with a slow-falling Senko, and they just can't resist taking an angry swipe.

If they ignore your offering on the drop, lightly twitch it back. Be forewarned—detecting these bites requires a sharp eye and sensitive touch. Watch your line (which probably is running slack) for any quiver, and monitor your rod tip closely on the pickup. If you feel any pressure, set the hook. Rather than striking this rig, they're inhaling it almost walleyelike. Nine out of 10 times, you won't feel anything until the hookset. When I first explain this to amateurs in the boat, I'll just tell them to "pick it up." If there's a fish there, great, but I don't want them wasting too much time trying to detect bites.

This weightless approach will work with other plastics, including your standard plastic worm. Just figure on using a smaller hook, say, 4/0 or 3/0. The thicker the plastic, the larger the hook or hook gap.

The wacky rig is so ridiculously simple. Via light line over clear water, this is an absolutely top technique. Know the water depth, and avoid letting the rig hit bottom—with that exposed hook, it will snag. (Weedless hooks are available and help here.) As you work it back up to the surface, shake

With a wacky rig, simply run the hook through the center of your Senko or other stickworm-style plastic. The action as this bait flutters toward the bottom drives bass nuts!

your rod tip to give the Senko some extra action. Also, know that bass have a tendency to tear wacky rigs apart. Be prepared to replace your soft stickbaits quite regularly with this technique.

Soft jerkbaits work in myriad other ways, too, from slow Texas rigging, to deadsticking, to drop-shotting, to a simple cast with a swimming retrieve. Because they're so thick and heavy, soft stickbaits can be fished weightless, which gives them an even, uniform horizontal fall fairly unique in the plastics world. They fall horizontally, and the ends flutter in a way bass can't resist. Pitch them under docks or cast them across narrow, underwater points and work them back.

Most bass anglers work soft stickbaits hard in the prespawn and postspawn period in semiweedy areas, but they'll perform the entire open-water season. Like other plastic baits, they come in every color of the rainbow, along with scented and salt-impregnated versions.

Spinnerbaits

Some old-timer tournament friends of mine lament the days before the spinnerbait hit the scene. I still remember the first time I saw someone in another boat pounding some big northern pike with a spinnerbait, then he began picking up lunker largemouths. I forget what I was using at the time, but it felt medieval compared to this bright, wiry, deadly contraption on the end of my friend's line. It seems as though aggressive presentations like spinnerbaits have lost a bit of their luster from fifteen to twenty years ago, but don't be fooled. Every bass tournament angler on the planet maintains a healthy arsenal of spinnerbaits in all shapes, colors, and sizes.

For covering water fast during an active bite, nothing else comes close to the deadly effective spinnerbait. You and a partner can fancast good-looking water with spinnerbaits that would take you many minutes with other lures. When prefishing a tournament, I've even thrown spinnerbaits without a hook. I'm not interested in lugging bass out of the water on prefishing days, so I'll confirm they're present (and build my confidence) via a few strikes on my hookless spinnerbaits, then return during the event with the real hooked deal or a finesse presentation. After testing a new location with a topwater lure (in the right conditions), spinnerbaits often are my second choice.

Unlike the plastics rig, which requires some time and failures to master, the spinnerbait is relatively idiot proof. A hardbait, it combines a flashy

Opposite: Spinnerbaits combine a jig with one or more blades to create one of the most versatile bass presentations on the water. They're available in hundreds, maybe thousands of variations, including the tandem-bladed willow design (top), single blade, and single rounded blade.

spinner to attract bass with the versatile and effective jighead via a tough metal wire. Tie it onto the end of some tough, braided line or heavier mono on your baitcasting rod, and you can horse a spinnerbait through the thickest weeds anywhere. The wire guard connecting the hook and skirt to the spinner blade assembly forces most weeds around anything that will snag. Spinnerbaits are great starter lures for first-timers or young anglers. Though most bass anglers run spinnerbaits fairly shallow, you can fish them in virtually any type of water—from shallow to deep, from ultraclear, to heavy vegetation, to downright muddy. Windblown shorelines, where wind-created current has congregated food sources, are great places to cast spinnerbaits tipped with a scented grub. Bass have the ability to locate the noise and pulse a big spinnerbait sends through the water column, even if low visibility prevents them from seeing it.

You can alter the look of a spinnerbait in innumerable ways. The parts on spinnerbaits are interchangeable, and you can easily purchase the components and switch them out quickly. Change the color of the skirt; the length of the skirt; or the size, shape, or number of blades. Throw a buzz spin onto it, and use it as a noisy topwater lure. For more noise, attach a rattling trailer onto the hook. Vary your retrieve so that it comes bouncing enticingly past a hungry largemouth, or burn it through the water column to trigger reaction strikes.

Want it to sink faster? Add a split-shot or two to the wire in front of the jighead. Give it a completely different look by dropping the skirt and reattaching a grub or short plastic finesse worm. Put the skirt on backward, and watch the bizarre look and action that gives it. Bass fishermen and women have been mixing and matching ideas for years with spinnerbaits, and I still believe we've only scratched the surface of these versatile lures.

When purchasing spinnerbaits, you should understand the basics of blades, which come in many different styles and colors. The blade is more than a visual attractor; it also creates vibration, which bass can sense from a long way via their sensitive lateral line. (Wounded baitfish toss and twist and create herky-jerky vibration, and in most cases we want our lures to do the same thing.) Willowleaf blades have, as their name implies, a longer, narrow profile that doesn't impart as much flash or pulse to the water, but they're also less likely to hang up in thick weeds.

In general, the more turbid the water, the bigger the blade. Tandem-bladed lures add a second blade for added flash for running through murkier

water or thicker vegetation. As far as color, I generally stick with silver in clearer water and then transition to gold as the water becomes more turbid; but I keep as many different shades in my tackle box as possible. I constantly experiment and try to forget the rules! Don't be afraid to purchase spinnerbaits with some wild and crazy colors. Although I have my favorite colors, especially white and green, I've never seen a color bass didn't like, including black.

Despite all the versatility, the lure still must remain in balance. Properly tuned, a spinnerbait should run with the blades on top and the jig and skirt running underneath in strike position. Banging a spinnerbait off rocks or docks can trigger strikes, but after a while it may knock the lure out of tune. Don't worry: With a basic set of needlenose pliers and a little trial and error, it's easy to bend it back into tune. Other factors, like an ultraheavy spinner, may overwhelm the rest of the lure so that it's out of tune and ends up rotating around the spinner. Wrong idea!

The water and structure I'm fishing will partially determine the type of rod and line I employ to fish spinnerbaits. When in doubt, I usually err on the side of finesse and run lighter, but the brilliance of a spinnerbait is that you can haul it through some serious thick stuff if you support it with a stout rod and heavy line. Whatever your rod-and-reel setup, be more concerned about presenting it delicately and quietly. If a harsh plop of your spinnerbait (or any lure) spooks every fish within striking distance, there won't be any hookset to worry about. Cast it lightly underhand so that the lure lands true, then jerk your rod tip to initiate the blades.

There are many different styles of retrieves, from blazing fast to slow and steady (which allows the spinnerbait to bounce along casually), and in tournaments I'm constantly altering how I reel. With any subsurface hard lure, especially spinnerbaits and crankbaits, a popular technique is purposely slamming it against a dock post, rock, or other hard object. The idea: We're trying to get the attention of a big bass with some noise and prompt a reaction strike. You can also work a spinnerbait like a jig with the old-reliable lift-drop retrieve we mastered back in the plastics section. In deeper water, especially adjacent to a drop-off structure, the falling spinnerbait performs what we seasoned bassers call a "helicoptering" effect, which gives the lure a different look and sometimes creates strikes. Sometimes I'll do this even in shallower water, just to change the look. In addition to varying the pace of your retrieve, you should also vary the

Opposite: You can find a crankbait to work nearly any portion of the water column. Deep divers have large front lips that force the lure farther underwater as you retrieve. Topwater cranks lack the lip but entice strikes from bass watching underneath.

depth—sometimes breaking the surface, sometimes running deeper. Have fun mixing it up.

Any time fish are in aggressive mood, spinnerbaits usually are my first choice. Shallow or deep, spinnerbaits are great for covering water. Obvious times include prespawn as the water begins to warm and autumn, when bass are wearing the feedbag. Late spring and early summer, before vegetation becomes too thick, also are good times.

Crankbaits

Like spinnerbaits, crankbaits qualify as hard baits, and they're extremely popular with anglers of all skill levels. Let's face it: They're cute! They resemble the baitfish we know predators want to consume, so logic dictates that bass will chase them, right? Well, not really. Crankbaits are mostly a reaction bait that prompts a chase response in the fish. Manufacturers market these smiling, clownish-looking lures as much to people as to fish, but you can't argue with their ability to catch multiple species—from walleyes and lake trout deep into the Great White North of Canada to lunker hawgs in Alabama or California.

Even more so than a spinnerbait, a crankbait allows you to cover serious water quickly and efficiently with a lifelike lure. You can fancast it to quickly explore new water, or—although more popular with pike, walleye, and muskie anglers—troll it. (Back in my early days of fishing, I trolled a few crankbaits dangling off the back of my canoe and had great fun.) You'll see several styles in this lure category: floaters, divers, and sinkers. Most crankbaits are made from wood and plastic, and you'll find that the most effective and popular crankbaits will gobble up a sizable portion of your wallet. You can spend $5 or $6 pretty easy for quality crankbaits, so these are the most expensive lures in your tackle box. Could be worse—muskie crankbaits cost even more!

During the past couple of decades, crankbaits have exposed an entire new fish zone to savvy bass anglers for the simple reason that they've boldly gone where no hard-bodied lure has gone before—deep water. Some anglers will even jam several feet of their rod underwater to help drive their lure even deeper. The secret to a crankbait's diving ability lurks mostly in its lip, though your choice in line and retrieval speed play a role here, too. Simple physics dictates that when you retrieve fast and pull hard on the nose of a big-lipped crankbait, it will dive deep—even to 16 or 18 feet. Some new

cranks on the market dive to a precise depth quickly and then remain at that level until they rise directly at boatside. (If possible, stick to reels with low gear ratios so that lures like these remain in the strike zone longer.) Lighter line gives you more control, and it will maximize the depth of the lure. Braided lines like Fireline really cut through the water and allow the lure to dive deeply, whether you're trolling or casting. (In clear water, however, always use a fluorocarbon leader when using a braided line—for stealth purposes.)

Tuned properly, the curved bodies of crankbaits wobble in the water column as you retrieve them. As with spinnerbaits, this creates that all-important pulse or vibration that entices fish in the vicinity that probably haven't seen your crankbait. When retrieving, if you feel that natural wobble cease, you've probably got a hit. One final wobble tip I've learned from my time on the water: Smallies prefer a smaller, narrower profile with less wobble; their largie cousins like fatter cranks with a big wobble.

Since a slow, steady retrieve best allows the crank's built-in action to perform, you can pretty much forget about all those nifty retrieval ideas from the spinnerbait section. That said, occasionally I'll employ a drag-and-reel pulsing-style retrieve just to mix things up (and work different muscles in my arms.) Also, the good old stop-and-go retrieve works really well with floating crankbaits, which will rise slowly when you stop reeling, then dive deeper again when you resume your retrieve. Seems like most hits occur just after you begin reeling.

Vegetation is to crankbaits as kryptonite is to Superman, and snagging even a small hunk of weeds will destroy a crankbait's performance until you can remove it. Thanks to a pair of big treble hooks dangling on your average crankbait, they grab anything they touch; therefore, we're using them mostly in weed-free situations. That said, cast parallel to a weed line, crankbaits produce fish. And if you just can't pass on tossing a crankbait toward some vegetation, a wider lip can help divert weeds and prevent hang-ups. They're ideal in hard-bottom situations or in flooded areas around stumps or other hard structures, like rocks or docks. As I mentioned in the spinnerbait section, try bumping cranks off hard structure to prompt reaction strikes. (Whenever you're fishing a hard lure, try to cast well past the "hot spot" where you believe fish will exist.) On sandy or mucky bottoms, I'll sometimes bump the crankbait on the bottom so that it kicks up a little sediment and gets the attention of large fish. To force it into the bottom, don't be afraid to add some weight. This is one reason I'll err on the side of a longer rod (7-footers) with crankbaits. That extra length helps you direct its pathway better, as well as providing better leverage if you snag up.

Lipless crankbaits, which include artificial lures like Berkley Rattlers, probably deserve their own category, but given the name, I'll discuss them here. They're a denser, thinner profile, flat lure that you cast and retrieve just as you would traditional round crankbaits. Especially early in the season, lipless cranks perform well when ripped quickly through light vegetation. Areas with early plant growth typically warm faster because they're shallower, so baitfish and bass frequent these areas, sometimes not long after ice-out (where bass seasons are open). They're a fun, more aggressive presentation during a time of year most anglers focus on finesse, but don't expect classic hard thumps from the bass. In my experience, early spring lipless crankbait strikes feel more like an added weight. If you feel any change in tempo to your retrieve, set the hook.

Lure companies construct crankbaits in every color or color combination that you can imagine, even holographic. When I'm fishing, I usually start with natural colors like perch or shad, but you'll find some pretty funky colors and rattling cranks in my tackle box, too. If there's a downside to crankbaits, it's that large bass have become conditioned not to strike some of them. On some of the potential "world record" reservoirs of California, I'm told hard-core bass anglers devise new and unusual lures to entice fish that have seen it all. Maybe that's why larger crankbaits tend to work better in spring than summer; it's been months since the fish have seen any lures move horizontally, so they're just a little dumber.

Although some bass anglers advocate strongly for using locking snaps to quickly change lures, I generally recommend tying directly onto the crank via the Palomar knot. The less fish-spooking hardware underwater, the better; plus it maximizes the lure's vibration and performance. Ironically, if a crankbait produces quick success on a spot, I'll reject it pretty fast if a couple more casts don't produce more action. Plastics usually produce bigger fish conditioned to avoid cranks, and once I know bass are present, I want to work the area thoroughly with slower presentations.

Jigs

Jig fishing might not garner the respect it deserves among rank-and-file anglers, perhaps because they demand more focus than other presentations. Nonetheless, they're great, versatile lures, especially in cooler water situations. Imagine a spinnerbait without the wire and blades, and you understand how a jig looks. As any self-respecting North Country walleye angler knows, a jig has a heavy, lead head painted in a bright color with a single hook underneath. For bass fishing, most have a skirt (hair, rubber, plastic, or silicone) and a weed guard over the hook so that you can fish them in pretty thick cover.

Many anglers combine a skirted jig with trailer of some sort—traditionally a chunk of pork rind, hence the name "jig-and-pig," or, more often nowadays, a grub or another plastic. Good old Uncle Josh Pork adds an enticing scent factor to the jig, although scented soft baits (especially craw-shaped) like Berkley Gulp! or salt-impregnated offerings now probably tip more jigs than pork products. I think the softer feel of the trailer, especially natural pork, entices bass to hold the lure longer, giving you more time to drive home the hookset. It may not be the best lure at all times, but it's rarely a bad option, especially when targeting big bass.

If you read closely throughout this section, you know that some lures perform better than others at certain depths: crankbaits deep, tubes shallow, and spinnerbaits somewhere in between. The versatile jig can cover each of those areas, plus they'll perform in multiple cover types—from weed beds, brush piles, logs, flooded brush, reeds, lily pads, and boat docks. I also like jigs because, unlike crankbaits or other more aggressive offerings, they're more forgiving in the constantly changing weather situations we see during the spring.

Early in the season, bass tend to be shallow because of the spawn. Most males will be defending the nests, and the females that have dropped their eggs and headed for nearby deeper water, usually not far away. They'll often hold on the first piece of structure, like a breakline, or around the edges of cover, like a weed bed. You can use jigs in either situation. For shallow bass, use a lightweight jig between ⅛ and ¼ ounce, with a trailer that matches the jig size. A larger trailer will help slow the jig's fall, but attach a trailer that's too big and it won't move realistically. It's important to maintain a deft touch on your line; in more challenging conditions, say, choppy water, you'll also need to increase jig weight.

Opposite: Throw a plastic skirt on a lead-headed hook, and you've got the popular and extremely effective skirted jig presentation. Note the thick, brushlike weed guard in front of the hook, which makes the jig relatively weedless and effective in vegetation.

In deeper water, say 12 to 15 feet, the same setup will work, except you should increase the weight of the jig to between ⅜ and ½ ounce to get deeper faster. In both scenarios, I'm using a long (at least 7 feet), medium-action rod with a braided line. If I switch to smaller jigs, I may switch to a lighter setup to better detect strikes, but generally we're targeting big fish, and I don't want to lose any in the weeds. Another caveat: In ultraclear water, I may use fluorocarbon simply because the fish are less likely to see it.

From a color standpoint, I prefer green pumpkin in clear water, black in darker water, and black and blue wherever bass swim. Many colors will perform, but as a general rule the more turbid or darker the water, the darker the lure. When I fish largemouth during the late evenings, you'll often find me using a dark-colored, rubber-skirted jig. A little noise doesn't hurt either in darker or murky water, so many of my jigs have rattles hanging from the hooks.

Properly working the lure is where the rubber meets the road with jigs, and here are some high-performance retrieve styles. Just as you would with a plastic rig, cast the jig to shallow cover and hop it slowly back to the boat. You're mimicking natural forage, like crayfish or large minnows, so under clear skies and in clear water, short, slower hops look more natural. All the hook-setting rules apply here: Watch and feel your line for any side-to-side movement or any subtle differences in how it moves. (There's another reason I use braided line: It's easier to see.) When something odd occurs, set the hook!

In shallow water, try "swimming" the jig back to the boat like a spinnerbait. Bass love spinnerbaits because they mimic natural baitfish, but they see a lot of them. Give bass a different choice, and even conditioned fish might just slam your lure. Keep your rod tip up and vary your retrieve—sometimes run it smooth; other times twitch it occasionally. A growing number of tournament anglers are employing this swimming technique later in the year to target suspended postspawn fish, particularly smallies. As summer progresses, begin targeting offshore structure, such as deep weed beds or underwater point or humps, with this swimming jig technique. Of course jigs are another obvious option for flipping under docks during the heat of late summer.

In my experience, jigs sacrifice numbers of fish but improve your odds of bigger fish, especially in deep water. As I've mentioned elsewhere in these pages, here's an obvious opportunity for deadsticking. Cast it to the bottom of the breakline, and then let it sit on the bottom. Occasionally twitch or shake it a bit. Drives bass nuts!

Jigs require patience, which I freely admit could probably rank higher on my personal list of virtues, but even I take my time with jigs because they're so darn effective. No, they're not as sexy as crankbaits, but you need to include jigs in your bass-fishing arsenal. Detecting bites can frustrate beginner bass anglers, but the only way to conquer that confusion is to get out and build jigging experience. As you pulse your jig across the bottom, pay close attention to how much weight it imparts into your rod. If it suddenly feels heavier or lighter, take up your slack line and set the hook. Finally, here's an idea that may sound like sacrilege in a bassin' book: Consider spending time with a seasoned jig-fishing walleye angler. A couple days hooking those subtle-biting fish will improve your understanding of bass strikes immensely.

Topwaters

OK, I really mean it this time: Topwater lures are my favorite way to catch bass! Unlike other underwater bassin' styles, topwater presentations occur on the surface, which allows us to use three senses: sight, sound, and touch. Those exciting, classic images of a massive largemouth erupting from the calm water and engulfing a poor, defenseless fishing lure usually involve a surface presentation. Such a scene demonstrates the awesome strength of bass, and with topwater it all occurs in plain view.

Whenever you see fish surface feeding or just breaking water, that's an obvious opportunity to throw a topwater lure in their direction. Prime topwater season for me occurs postspawn, when the water temperatures are beginning to warm but remain cool compared to the heat of summer. Fish are tired and unwilling to chase a bigger, faster presentation like a spinnerbait or crankbait. They're hungry and becoming more aggressive, but the more subtle action of a topwater lure can elicit strikes. Later in summer, suspended bass in deep water will attack a popper or other topwater lure, and I'll work these lures over the shallows again in the fall. Prime hours for casting a topwater lure are early mornings and evenings over a calm, still surface. In river situations, try to find slackwater areas where the action of a topwater lure really shines.

A number of specific lures fall under the heading of topwater: poppers/ chuggers, spoons and frogs, stickbaits, jerkbaits, buzzbaits, and propbaits.

As you retrieve a popper lure, its blunt front end imparts noise and a bubble trail that bass find irresistible. The herky-jerky action probably mimics a wounded fish or amphibian, which spells "easy meal" to a hungry bass.

Though different in appearance and how you'll retrieve them, most float. Buzzbaits, which look like a funky spinnerbait, are an exception to that rule. Their big blades act as little propellers to churn the water while you reel. Predatory fish see and hear their action and think "wounded baitfish on the surface!" Hauled over even the thickest weeds bed, they're great bass attractors; just make sure you keep your rod tip up and vary your retrieve as much as possible. Adding a trailer of some sort can boost the scent factor.

Stickbaits are my favorite style of topwater fishing, and a Zara Spook probably best represents the category. Saltwater and freshwater anglers alike have enjoyed great sportfishing via the simple lure, which requires you to impart action with simple starts, jerks, and pauses. When you hear the phrase "walk the dog" in bass fishing, tourney anglers usually are talking about this back-and-forth action of stickbaits. You also can deadstick, which we've mostly suggested on the bottom—except with stickbaits, it happens at the surface. Cast it out, reel a few feet, and then stop. Take a sip of coffee, check your bearings, clear out a backlash, or just do something that forces you not to twitch or touch that lure for twenty to thirty seconds. Then resume, and you'll be amazed at how often you get a strike. If you see a fish's wake behind your lure, but it won't strike, reel

faster. Bam, that lunker probably will strike hard. If they miss it on the first strike, slow down and keep working it; the fish may take a second or even third swipe. Stickbaits are more of a mid- to late-summer lure for me, and they deliver in open water or around structure like docks, stumps, or over weed beds. Over real clear water, I'd probably start with a stickbait, since they're the subtlest of the topwater presentations.

The difference between a hard-bodied jerkbait and a stickbait probably strikes most new anglers as pretty subtle. Jerkbaits look like slender, longer crankbaits and perform much the same way, except they're surface oriented. They're light, float, and provide us with a more subtle way to impart action on a hard-bodied lure than the traditional casting-and-wheeling style of using a crankbait. They're a great deadsticking surface lure.

Poppers or chuggers are somewhere in between the previous examples in that, like buzzbaits, they make their own noise and action, yet you can retrieve them in the same manner as a stickbait with a pause-start, pause-start cadence. Even beginner anglers have probably heard of a jitterbug—perhaps the best-known popper-style lure. Their blunt, angled heads result in an uneven retrieve that causes them to jump, or "pop," while you reel. This creates herky-jerky, noisy movement and bubbles that—again—probably mimic a wounded baitfish or amphibian. For a big bass, that spells

How any fish can stop itself from striking a Super Spook "walked" back to the boat, I will never know. Walking the dog with a topwater stickbait is my favorite style of bass fishing. You can't beat the excitement when a massive bass envelops a topwater with a water-erupting boil.

lunch. Again, patience is a virtue; let the popper rest a bit, and wait. Fly-anglers use small poppers but follow the same retrieve principles. Hook a 3-pound smallie on a 5-weight fly rod, and you're in for a wild ride!

Propbaits, including my personal favorite, the wooden Smithwick Devil's Horse, have a funny little propeller on their nose and tail. I like to throw propbaits (and stickbaits) because it seems that bass prefer longer, thinner lures. Don't get me wrong. There are days when short, fat cranks are the only presentation that will produce, but long and thin generally has been more productive for me over the years. Prime time for propbaits occurs after the water has warmed, and every time I tie one of these, I can't help but think of the stereotypical image of a geeky propellerhead. But that's not to disrespect propbaits, which—as you retrieve them—create a churning "whoosh-whoosh" sound in the water to attract predators. You can work these torpedo-shaped lures slow or fast, but remember to allow long pauses when retrieving them. Immediately after you cast, let the ripples dissipate before reeling.

Weedless spoons and artificial frogs don't generate quite the attention from bass anglers that they did years back. Over thick lily pads (or even if allowed to sink through submerged weeds), however, both can still produce, perhaps because fewer anglers are throwing these lures anymore. A black or silver Johnson's minnow (spoon) with a chunk of pork rind skipped over the lilies sure looks enticing to me, and I usually keep a rod equipped with heavy braided line on hand for the job. A stiff metal weed guard keeps these lures fairly weedless. Pull a spoon or frog onto a big lily pad for a moment, then lightly pull it into adjacent water. That's often when the strike will occur. Like I said, I don't catch a lot of bass like this, but when I do, it's a blast.

Now let's talk a little about the hookset with surface lures. Since your first reaction when a lunker grabs for your lure is to rear back, use a medium-action rod when working topwater lures to tone that back a bit. Stay patient, and allow the bass to engulf your lure before setting the hook; but if you still drive the hook-set too early, a faster tip gives you a little room for error. Apply the same hookset rules you would with an underwater lure: Determine when to set the hook by feel, not by sight.

In the color category, I'll start fishing with perch or shad, but in a tournament situation, I keep the full color spectrum of lures available.

Topwater poses a simple line and equipment dilemma. Our gear demands some toughness, given that a big largie will head toward China (and the thickest cover in between) once he grabs our lure. That said, long casts past key structure targets are all-important, too. I use the lightest line possible—say, twelve-pound test for those lighter lures—and then play the fish high in the water column. To deliver maximum action on my topwater lures, I prefer medium- to heavy-action 7-foot rods. The thicker the slop, the heavier the action.

Early in the year, I hope for prime topwater conditions, but if these lures don't perform on a given day, I don't hesitate to switch to a spinnerbait or maybe a floating crankbait; the latter allows me to work that same slow, let-it-sit-a-few-seconds retrieve.

CHAPTER FOUR

Which Technique When

Now that we've talked technique, let's talk about which technique to use at what time during what I'd like to call "A Year in the Life of the Average Bass." Actually, we're only going to focus on the open-water season, but I think you get the picture. When the ice disappears in the middle or northern portion of the country, we bass anglers are ready to hit the water. Here are my thoughts on where we'll find bass on any given day, depending on the season.

Prespawn and Spawning

Early in the year—after ice-out in some states or around "opener" in places like my own Minnesota—I usually focus on muddy or, more appropriately, turbid bays and coves. The water has warmed faster here than in clear water, so we've got a better chance of encountering postspawn fish during the early bass season. Turbid water holds more heat, so it holds more baitfish, too. Another tip: South-facing bays will warm faster than north-facing bays. Especially early in the season, the bass aren't in the shallows strictly to spawn, although the males already are sniffing around for good bedding sites. But they're mostly hungry and following those forage sources. It's a good time for topwater presentations, especially in wind-protected bays or the leeward side of points. Early-season crappie and panfish anglers in the upper Midwest frequently bump into bass when chasing the slabs in these locations during early May, or even late April.

We're looking for a temperature in the low 60-degree range for spawning to begin. Largemouth begin spawning around 60 degrees, so I usually consider water above 63 degrees postspawn. Food takes a backseat to spawning now, though the males especially are protective of the beds and are in pretty shallow—less than 10 feet—water. Once bass begin spawning, they're pretty darn easy to catch. Generally speaking, I discourage fishing bass on the beds because it's not much of a challenge, and probably not good for the species. Pull a hovering papa bass off the bed as he tries to guard the eggs, and we risk allowing bluegills or other fish to eat the eggs. That can't be good for bass or bass fishing. If you do decide to spend a little time targeting these fish, use artificial lures to avoid gut-hooking the fish, then return them to the water quickly. Fish may venture out of the area immediately after the spawn, but I firmly believe that some big fish forage around shallow water structure year-round.

Postspawn

OK, the term "postspawn" has a certain, frankly undeserved negative connotation. If you're a parent, it's easy to imagine a lethargic mom or pop largemouth, finished with a couple weeks' worth of giving birth (laying eggs in mom's case) then defending the kids from the local punk bullies (big panfish). All they want to do is recuperate out of harm's way (the local breakline) and chill out! No eating, no fighting, no sniffing your lures, just resting. Well, it's not quite that bad, for a couple of reasons. For one, the postspawn period when females recover and males complete defending the nests only lasts about a week. For two, postspawn lethargy is overplayed; we can still catch bass at this time. They'll remain in the vicinity of the beds but hang out near that deeper-water breakline for much of the day for security, although much of their—albeit limited—feeding will occur in the shallows. Females leave the bedding area first, then the males follow a few days to a week later.

Obvious structure to target for fishing is drop-offs, inside breakline turns with rock and cabbage, points, and shallow docks adjacent to deeper depths. Always check weed edges! View these weed edges as highways from the spawning areas to deepwater summer haunts. Unique bottom structure like rock piles or sudden holes serve almost as stop signs along the way. In short, postspawn bass usually return to the same locations where we found them prior to the spawn to recover, then they'll spread out to slightly deeper water and structure.

I thoroughly fish rocky, weedy points, rock piles, and hard-bottom areas; baitfish will key on these areas.

Early Summer

Some of the best fishing of the season occurs during this time, as bass are ready to actively feed and resume the life of the freshwater piscatorial world's biggest little toughies. Everything is coming together to provide prime time for pursuing bass. They're hungry and over the postspawn blues. New plant growth has oxygenated the water nicely, and we've got an abundance of baitfish and insects emerging into the waterways. In many portions of the country, bass haven't seen an artificial lure for many months, so they're willing to slam your lures.

When working the early-summer period, monitor the bottom and weed structure as you enter the bay or cove. That milfoil or other structure at 3 to 5 feet coming off the main lake could be extremely productive. Once I'm deeper into the bay, I'll concentrate on the weed line near shore or any downed trees. Don't be afraid to key on early lily pads. They sometimes produce a fish.

As bass begin transitioning into that active, early-summer feeding phase, this is a great time for crankbaits. Also, via relatively light line in the ten- to twelve-pound-test range, use light sinkers ($\frac{1}{16}$-ounce or smaller) and a variety of plastics, such as crayfish, spider-type grubs and tubes—these are prime lures for spring bass. I've found a lot of success early in the summer with a slow-falling plastic rig for triggering strikes.

Late Summer

We have a couple of other factors working against us in late July and early August. First, the spawn ended at least a month or two earlier, and that postspawn feeding period has waned. Second, baitfish are everywhere. This isn't cold, void, unproductive early-season water. Small panfish and other baitfish have been proliferating for months and provide a steady, natural food source for predators like bass. Also, the shallows have warmed to the point that they're becoming uncomfortable to big bass under a high sun, so we're less likely to find them in those relatively easy-to-locate early-season haunts.

But we have several factors working for us. Bass are less active than they were a month ago, or will be again in early autumn, but in this warm water we've struck the heart of the growing season. Bass are feeding in midsummer, even in the shallows early and late in the day. Second, the fish may be more concentrated now than at any other time during the open-water season. During the middle portion of the day, they'll even school up off the breakline and around deeper structure. Third, because of the sometimes daunting conditions—i.e., heat and humidity—of dog days fishing, bass see less fishing pressure late in the summer than in June or early July.

For the above reasons, late-summer bass fishing usually shakes out as either really good or really bad. We can sum up location with one spot: deepwater weed lines over hard bottoms. Using your electronics, work that outside weed edge, which typically sets anywhere from 12 to 20 feet.

I'll start with crankbaits as a search tool or, if there are two people in the boat, have one person work a spinnerbait, just to mix things up. Use natural-colored cranks (remember all those new baitfish?) in perch, shad, or crawdad (crayfish) colors first.

Sometimes it takes a pass or two to learn the lay of the weed line. Watch your depthfinder to keep the boat just off the edge of the heavy weeds so that you're not wasting time clearing lures. That said, if you're pulling coontail off your lures, you're in the right place. Bass love the stuff.

Once you've nailed down the weed line location, a deep-diving crankbait works well because it gets down fast and covers a lot of water in the strike zone. Work those heavy spinnerbaits the same way, a technique bass geeks call "slow rolling." After your cast, let it settle to the bottom, give it a quick pump to activate the blades, then reel it in real slow. You're trying to keep it in the strike zone as long as possible.

Thoroughly fish weed points, rocky points, rock piles, and any hard-bottom areas. Baitfish will key on these areas, and so will the bass. Watch the surface. If you see panfish or other baitfish breaking the surface, there's a good chance a school of largemouth are feeding underneath. That's a key word here: *school*. Bass actually school up and concentrate off these deep weed lines in late summer. If you find one, you'll usually find a whole pod. After two or three strikes or releases on my search baits, I've found the school and will begin altering tactics. I'll switch to jig-and-pig or a jig and plastic. Employ a skirted jig with a weed guard, and tip it with something tasty, like a plastic trailer, salt craw, or Berkley power craw. Go ahead and try a Texas rig if you prefer—say, with a 7-inch turtleback worm or on a ⅛- to ⅜-inch jig.

When you discover a good school of bass, you can create an almost frenzied feeding (and thus fish-catching) scenario. Multiple strikes and hooked hawgs roaring to and from the boat stir up the baitfish, which in turn whip up other bass. Within seconds, you'll have the same wild-eyed grimace when you're connecting with fish every other cast.

Early Autumn

September is the second best time for fishing bass across the northern United States—after that all-important postspawn period in early June (in places like Minnesota). That statement carries an important caveat: After August fish begin to scatter, so you'll find fewer pods of largemouth. Turnover occurs in late September, and bass literally could be anywhere in the lake. Finding these fish is a challenge. Turnover occurs when layers of warm and cool water flip, usually in late September. A warm top layer that developed over the summer cools off quickly with autumn's cold evenings and eventually flips and mixes with the colder layer underneath. The mixing and chaos that occurs when the lake bottom waters rise to the top throws fish off, and pretty well trashes the bites, for upwards of a week. Once the water temperatures become consistent through midfall, bass reactivate for a great bite until really cold weather arrives. Then bass enter a cold-water lethargic funk that sends most hard-core bassers toward California or southern climes until ice-out the following spring.

But between turnover and ice, we can enjoy the great late season. The days are getting shorter, the mornings a little cooler, and bass—like their human counterparts—have the desire and energy to hunt. The harshest, strongest strikes of the year will occur during this time.

So let's tackle the challenging part of early-fall fishing equation: the search. You just read a simple rule for August bass—deep weed lines. That location and those tactics would still work if not for one little problem: The weed lines aren't there anymore. OK, that's a slight exaggeration. The weeds still exist, but some, especially the cabbage, have died back significantly by now. That means less oxygen, which is less desirable for baitfish. You know the rest by now: No baitfish, no bass.

Weeds begin greening up in May and early June in the northern United States and peak by mid-July. By late July, depending on lake clarity and bottom content, some weeds will be dying back, especially in the shallows. Bass have fewer ambush points in dying weeds, so they'll seek whatever green weeds remain. So in late summer, start there. Dig out some topwaters, watch the surface for baitfish, and cast around some heavy weed beds. Start with surface lures, then transition to jig-and-pigs. As astute readers know, I love plastics, but I find myself switching more to active lures like spinnerbaits in 8 to 10 feet of water. Remember, those wild-eyed bass are more apt to hit now because Mother Nature is telling them that winter is coming; that triggers feeding and more strikes.

When you find bass, expect quality fish in the 3- to 3½-pound range. You'll find scattered fish and fewer schools, but the quality should be pretty good. They've nearly completed an entire growing season, so they're fat and healthy. This is the time of year that state records are broken. When you find a weed pattern, it should run fairly consistent throughout the lake. A mix of green cabbage (if any still exists) and coontail is my favorite place to start.

No luck with that weed pattern? Don't give up, because here's another autumn location. Let's say things have progressed further than we first thought, and the fish are moving deeper already. In southern reservoirs, while we anglers in the North are fishing the hard water, jigging spoons are a winter bass bite lure. They'll drop them down 30 or 40 feet and jig-crank it like an ice walleye bite. Now, I'm not suggesting we employ that technique during an autumn in Minnesota or New York, but we can intercept the bass on their way to winter haunts. How? By fishing vertical, deep drops.

Deepwater breaks, especially near heavy weed flats, are one of my favorite areas in late September. Use your electronics to locate baitfish schooled on these areas. This could be over water as deep as 25 to 30 feet. Early in the day, I'll often find bass near the edge of a break, then they'll transition deeper later in the day. Toss out a jig worm with a jig, say about $3/32$ ounce. (I'm a firm believer in the lighter, the better.) Bite off half an inch of that 7-inch plastic worm, or try the same jig with a Senko. Cast it toward the break, and follow the top line back down. Even in autumn, quite often all you'll feel is extra weight when the strike occurs. Watch your line for a flick or jump, and set the hook.

Want one more, exciting option? Target the frog migration! All those amphibians are moving around and heading for the shallows to settle in for winter. Work the surviving lily-pad fields near swampy or boggy areas for bass chasing small frogs. Start with a jig-and-pig in a black-and-blue, ½- to ¾-ounce jig, with a black/blue trailer. This is a bit like dipping milfoil. You're making short casts, even pitching, not far from the boat in about 5 feet of water. Bites will be fewer and farther between using this tactic, but when they hit, you'll know it. Maybe try that black Johnson's minnow and pork frog, too.

The conditions in autumn demand versatility. Come fall, you'll find me in many lake locations chasing bass, even casting to the occasional dock if any green weeds remain in the vicinity.

It's a great time of year for catching bass. You can even sleep in a bit, since the colder water means a later bite. Yeah, they're scattered, but when you find 'em, their aggressive attitude will remind you of why we call them hawgs.

River Bass Fishing

Before moving on to destinations, I want to spend some time on a couple of exceptions to the rules. First, don't forget rivers; second, what to do in a real tough bite situation. Let's start with moving water.

Too often in the Midwest or Northeast, people dismiss rivers for bass fishing. There's the occasional smallmouth article with some fly-rod-wielding yuppie targeting those trendy bronzebacks on a scenic stream, but that's about it. Yet seasoned bass anglers know that rivers contain—pound for pound—some of the strongest largemouth bass in the country.

River fishing scares some people, and I admit that when I started, fishing big currents scared me, too. On big rivers like the Mississippi, you're dealing with lots of current, huge barges, and wing dams that can destroy your lower unit. It's intimidating to a first-timer, and you've got to be careful! Now I've fished a number of big waters, including the St. Lawrence Seaway (where there are some really huge ships), and I respect big waters instead of fearing them. In fact, I've learned to love big rivers.

Believe it or not, rivers give flatland anglers a taste of saltwater fishing sometimes 1,000 or more miles from the coast. Ever fished salt water? All those tidal forces and currents running every which way (not to mention lots of toothy predators chasing one another around) create remarkably strong, resilient fish. They're unrelenting swimmers with unbelievable

By understanding the life cycles of bass, we can enjoy good fishing for the species during the entire open-water season. Prime times to work shallow water structure for north country largemouth (shown) typically occur in early summer or early autumn.

endurance. River fish, like their saltwater comrades, are survivors. Burning those extra calories fighting current means river species forage more often and more aggressively than their slackwater counterparts. Bass can be tougher to pattern in rivers because of this constant foraging, but if you adjust your tactics accordingly, you'll find 'em. For starters, spend more time with active presentations like crankbaits, and place less emphasis on finesse lures like plastics.

Prime spring conditions for river-fishing bass usually start with long, gradual snowmelt and stable crests. Unlike a year with flood conditions, which scatter fish, in low-water years river largemouths are more predictable

and easier to locate. Because the water warms faster in rivers than in lakes, river bass spawn up to a month earlier than their lake cousins. When the temperature hits 57 degrees in a river, bass start spawning. In most rivers across the northern tier of the United States, they'll wrap it up by late April or early May, whereas you're looking at June in a lot of lakes.

You'll often find smallmouth and largemouth bass in the same rivers. Follow the same rule you would on a lake: Smallies suspend more around gravel and rock, while largemouth inhabit the softer bottom areas (where there's less current). Postspawn, work vegetation and, especially early in the year, shallow, slackwater areas. We're talking 1 to 5 feet of water with a little of that precious forage-carrying current. Toss a buzzbait or spinnerbait in there, and work it back slowly and erratically.

In late May on big rivers, focus on wing dams, particularly spots where you can find a break. Occasionally a barge or towboat will bump the rocks underneath and create an opening. Largemouth bass hunker down in these breaks (commiserating with those pesky walleyes), and as the current washes minnows through, the bass gobble them up. Stay right above the breaks, and drop a tube jig. This is fun fishing!

The tough part is keeping your boat over the right spot. Spend some time studying your electronics and learning a specific wing dam top to bottom. You can also try casting spinnerbaits to shore and working them back over the wing dam. Remember, this is stained water, so flash is important. Use a No. 5 or 7 willowleaf or larger on your spinnerbait in gold or copper. If you're a late riser, you'll love river largemouth fishing. The bite seems to peak mid- to late morning, so I rarely hit the water before 8:30 or 9:00 a.m. The turbid, stained water of North Country rivers seems to mean these fish hunt best in strong daylight when they can see forage.

One of my partners a couple of years back accused me of only wanting to fish smallmouth on rivers. Upon further review: Guilty as charged. I guess the kid in me just gravitates toward those river smallies, even if it sometimes means hitting the water earlier than the average bear.

Wind plus current can equal some massive, powerful wave action. Be prepared for it, and be willing to move if it makes conditions unfishable. In a tournament with high current a few years ago, the wind and current were simply too strong. By slowly snaking my way through little channels, I found places with inlets where I felt comfortable. Obviously, be careful under such unfamiliar conditions. Once you wreck your boat, you can't fish.

But that said, I love river fishing. Again, just like salt water, you never know what you're going to catch in a river—thumping catfish, American eel, even sturgeon! And those big barges or ships I mentioned earlier? They stir up the shad, which in turn stirs up a mini feeding frenzy. And you can't beat an angry, hungry largemouth who's been fighting current all day.

Energizing a Slow Bite

Every angler—winter or summer, hard water or soft water—has experienced "the lost bite." Fish were slamming your lure yesterday, but twenty-four hours later—in identical conditions—you can't buy a strike. What's going on? First, let me assure you, such scenarios frustrate anglers of all levels, amateur and professional alike. While prefishing Lake Champlain in upstate New York/Vermont in September 2005, my co-angler and I enjoyed an absolutely fabulous smallmouth bite. Three- and 4-pounders were slamming a green-skirted spinnerbait and a chartreuse crankbait off a deep flat.

Believe it or not, my partner and I were searching for places where the fish weren't biting, just to mix up our tactics. Bottom line, it was one of the best fishing days of my life. Bet you know where this is going, right? Tournament day arrived forty-eight hours later, and the conditions looked identical: heat, dead calm, and sunny, clear skies. Yet I could not find a bite in the same locations with those two lures. The dominant thought in my head that day: They're gone!

The smallies hadn't evacuated the area. They still were there (or at least very close), but they didn't want what I was offering anymore. Here's how I salvaged the day.

One glance around the lake (many other teams were working the same flat) showed little casting occurring. Call me stubborn, but I just didn't want to adjust. Finally, I switched to a less-aggressive, tube jig presentation. Suddenly, on the same waypoints, I began catching smallies. They were in little schools, and good fishing commenced.

Two learning experiences from the day: First, being stubborn never pays off. Second, don't think just because fish aren't biting that they're not present.

In this Lake Champlain example, there was a perfectly legitimate reason the bite switched. Yeah, the conditions were identical to forty-eight hours earlier, but during the day in between, a big wind had whipped up the lake. It even kept me off the water for most of the day. Throw in several hundred hours of hard-core prefishing bassers on Champlain, and the smallies wanted a more casual dining experience! I thought the lake had settled down from the wind and pressure. It hadn't.

After the yank-your-arm-off experience of prefishing, shifting my mindset toward a more patient presentation demanded serious effort. I had no patience for a wacky- or straight-hooked worm. Slowing down wasn't easy, but it ultimately paid off. Here's a simple protocol for when you find yourself in a similar situation on local water.

Many factors can alter a hot bite: hot weather, cold fronts, big winds, no wind, fishing and boating pressure, and changing water levels. If a bite changes, take a hint from the fish, and take it quickly. First, use and trust your electronics. In the 12-foot water over this flat, we could see fish on the graph. That encouraged us to switch tactics until we found success. If they're gone, let the search commence. Start at the break—that neutral zone where stressed fish inevitably retreat.

Start slow. A simple finesse worm is my favorite—go worms for largies, tubes for smallies. A weighted jig with a nice steady fall ranks pretty high on my bassing repertoire during a tough bite. Work with your fishing partner(s) to mix it up. Maybe your buddy fancasts a search bait—a spinnerbait, rattler, or shallow-diving crank—to find active fish, while you stick with a slower presentation, like a wacky rig. Nothing doing? Work deeper. A rule of thumb: Deeper fish demand a more precise presentation, so work slowly and methodically. If nothing's happening deep, move to the shallows fast, especially early in the season.

In really shallow water (where bass anglers often find themselves), you can't see fish on screen because they're not under the boat. Throw all manner of search baits—topwater, divers, and spinners until one of you finds an active fish. Then at least one of you should revert to a slower-action lure until you find the magic bullet. Or take my advice from earlier, and pursue river-dwelling fish, which seem less susceptible to changes in weather, or whatever, affecting their behavior. Maybe it's because they cope with currents and a steadier diet of fluctuating conditions.

Sharp changes in weather aren't mandatory to shut down a bite. All these rules apply during transition times of year: spring or fall, or around the spawn. People and their attempts to improve lakes can alter the bite, too. In 2006 I enjoyed fantastic fishing on a metro area lake—we're talking a consistent catch of 3- to 5-pound fish off the weed line. Then the city or a local lake association sprayed the weed line, and the fish disappeared.

I searched and worked different spots via multiple presentations, and nothing. They didn't die, because I didn't see (or smell) rotting bass along shore, but I never did find those fish. Frankly, it bugged me all winter. Chemical spraying onshore or in the water can affect fish behavior. So can weed harvesting. Think all that milfoil cutting occurring on some lakes doesn't alter bass behavior?

Don't let a tough bite ruin your fishing. Chalk it up the challenge of fishing, then let the modern tactics and tools of twenty-first century fishing lead you to the promised bite!

CHAPTER FIVE

Bass Fishing Dilemmas ... and How I Solved Them

Let's spend a few pages solving some fishing dilemmas and quandaries that I've faced during my fifteen years of tournament fishing. Think of them as mini-mysteries involving uncooperative bass. By following the clues we've already learned and thinking outside the box, we'll put them in the boat. I've learned a lot about fishing bass from these anecdotes, and you will, too.

Double-Strikers

Once, while fishing a tournament in the Thousand Islands chain in the St. Lawrence River, I was finding success working Senkos on the inside weed lines. Working my way along, I eventually cast adjacent to a log, had a good strike and followed with a solid hookset. Somehow, however, the line broke—probably because that big fish wrapped around a branch. Now, a lot of people believe that a fish in that situation wouldn't strike again—maybe for days. Wrong!

I switched to a skirted jig-and-pig, and then flipped it to the exact same spot. Bam! When I got that 4-pound largie to the boat, my Senko was still in its mouth. That fish was hiding in there, waiting for forage to float past in an eddy's light current just off the main river. He wanted something in his face, and that combination connected. The situation reinforced a simple rule of bass fishing: If you miss a fish once, give it a whirl with something different. Bass will strike multiple times.

Lure Size Matters

Lure size can be key to catching fish, and here's an example: Early in my tournament-fishing career, I participated in an event on North South Center Lake in the Chisago Lakes region northeast of the Twin Cities. I was having a lot of luck catching 2-pound bass via a jig worm. It started out as great fun, but after catching a dozen 2-pounders, I realized my total weight was remaining static. A live well full of 2-pounders won't win many tournaments.

Then a little voice reminded me of another good bassin' rule: If you want bigger fish, try a bigger lure. There may be bigger fish among smaller ones, and they may prefer something larger. Don't get me wrong here. Large fish will take smaller lures, too, but on some days small may not be worth a big fish's time. In a school of smaller fish, try a larger lure. It worked on North South Center that day: I went from a ⅛- to a ½-ounce jigging worm and almost immediately caught two 4-pounders that put me "in the money" at that event.

I run four basic lure groups (albeit with plenty of deviations, as you've seen throughout these pages): spinnerbaits, jerkbait, topwaters, and plastic—tubes, grubs, and worms. Keep them in multiples sizes in your tackle box, from ⅛ ounce to ½ ounce, and be willing to upsize, even when you're catching fish.

Lure "Chumming"

OK, so my fishing partner Howie and I are working the smallmouth on Lake Vermillion in northeastern Minnesota. Jerkbaits were producing slow but fairly steady action in the cool water, and we realized that entire schools of smallies were following our lures back to the boat. We were getting few hits, and most hooksets involved smaller fish.

Then Howie fashioned a plan: One of us should toss a tube just past the point where the schools would back off our jerkbait. Offer them something different before they moved back to the safety of the weed line. It worked! We took turns alternating between attracting the fish with our topwaters, then hammering the big ones—cast after cast—with tube jigs. We joked that we were chumming with artificial lures, but the experience brought home an important lesson for me: Whenever possible, work together with your fishing companions, and you may both enjoy the fruits of your cooperation.

Postspawn Blues

After the spawn, when large females head for the first weed lines, bass have a reputation for being ridiculously lethargic. Two years ago, while prefishing an early-June event on Lake Minnetonka, I was swimming jigs against the inside weed line. Fish were active and biting, but twenty-four hours later—day one of the tournament—nada. The fish had finished spawning, and they were tired and lethargic.

Howie and I were marking fish and tried everything from every angle before finally hitting a successful technique. We faced the weed line from deeper water and wacky rigged. We literally had to spoon-feed those lethargic big mommas and cast from a long ways for stealth. First we thought weightless, but that wasn't working. We needed to toss it directly in the weeds, right in front of the fish, and that required a weedless hook. Lethargic yes, but they'd eat something tantalizing right in front of them. An amazingly productive day of fishing ensued, and my fishing partner and I "cashed a check." Every year since at that event (and a few others), I catch fish in there at that time. The message here: A slowly worked wacky rig is irresistible for lethargic postspawn fish.

Opposite: Artificial frogs work great through thick vegetation and mimic an obvious bass food source. Don't be surprised if other species, like pike or muskies, take a swipe at this realistic offering.

Frog Success

Spring 2007 brought me to a chunk of water I'd never fished before: the Potomac River along Maryland, Virginia, and the Washington, D.C., area. In the Upper Midwest we have loads of milfoil, and it runs deeper than what I encountered in this East Coast waterway. Don't ask me why, but it stops at 5 to 6 feet deep in the East, whereas it runs in excess of 10 feet deep back home.

I don't fish many artificial frogs in northern climes, but I've used them extensively on the Potomac this spring and found great success in the weeds. A nifty trend has developed that's worth sharing. Over deeper water, I'm throwing bigger artificial frogs over the tops of matted weeds and getting strikes. On shallower water, fish don't like those big, noisy lures, but smaller, soft horny toads are nabbing largies. The combination of light current, shallow water, and healthy weed beds has created the successful formula, and I can't wait to employ this back home in summer.

Changing Patterns

In August 2006 on Lake Minnetonka, a fishing partner and I ran smack into a nasty weather change. Our prefishing produced lots of healthy bass in the milfoil in some high-70s-/low-80s-temperatures. The tournament starts, and sweltering mid-90s heat and bright skies arrive. Despite the weather change, we started where we found success, by flipping the foil with heavy jigs. Where we'd been catching fish like crazy the previous two days, we now found ourselves catching one here, one there at a gruelingly slow rate under that beastly sun.

Our initial thought was that the bass had moved shallower but deeper into the thick foil for protection from the direct sunlight. No dice. So we figured, if they're not on the weed edge and not shallow, they must have gone deeper. We went to the first, nearest structure we could find, some rocks at about 20 feet deep, and cast with Carolina rigs. Sitting off in deeper water, we cast to the weed edge and began retrieving. Just as we could feel it leaving the weeds, strike!

My partner switched to a bare (as opposed to skirted) football-shaped head with a crayfish-shaped, twin-tailed Yamamoto plastic. He'd let it get

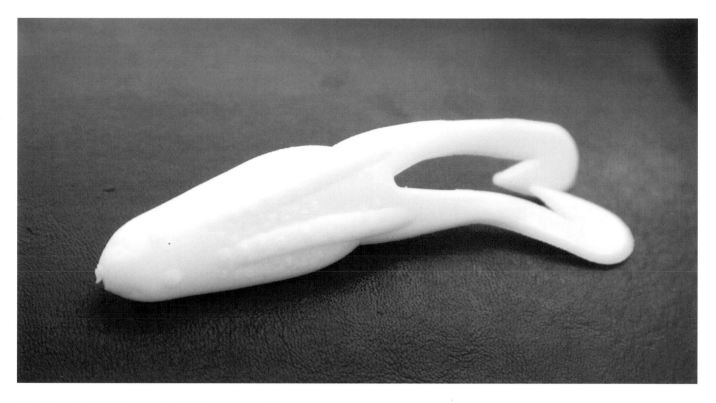

stuck for a moment in the rocks, then tease it loose to impart some killer crayfishlike action as it bounced over the rocks. Drove them nuts!

We solved this puzzle at about 11:00 a.m., and spent the remainder of the day working the pattern. Occasionally we'd try flipping the foil again, but it continued to stink, so we quickly returned to the rocks. Our final tally didn't win the tournament, but it put us in the money.

The moral of this story? He (or she) who isolates the pattern first in a tournament situation usually comes out on top. If you find fish one day, but then temperatures or conditions change, the fish aren't far away. Consider what happened here. Given the heat, my personal guess was that they went deeper. I suspect that had it been just bright sunshine, they would have headed for weeds; but it was heat and sun, so they went deeper. We had no time to search for fish somewhere else, so we went to deep spots nearby. The pattern changed, so we changed, too.

CHAPTER SIX

Fourteen Prime Bass Destinations

So, we've described all of my favorite pro tactics for fishing bass. Now the powers that be want me to tell you where to employ these techniques. I've fished hundreds of lakes and rivers, so it is with some trepidation that I've agreed to select my top 14 bass-fishing destinations across the United States and Canada. Choosing such a list has a bit of an elitist vibe to it, and that's something I've tried to avoid throughout these pages. Bass fishing belongs to Americans of all shapes, creeds, and colors: They're the common woman's fish, readily available in small lakes and ponds across the country, and that's why we love them so much. Nonetheless, I think sharing some destinations has merits on two counts.

First, if you really get into bass fishing (which I'm confident many of you will), then you may enjoy traveling to new, unusual, or otherwise interesting places to find these species. The list I'll unveil in this section contains some beautiful, historic country that's worth visiting, so even if the bass decide not to bite during your visit, you'll enjoy some fabulous scenery. Americans love to travel, so why not tow the boat and hit some of these prime bass-fishing spots while you're on the road?

The second reason is that even though many of these places may not make your list of travel destinations, I believe you still can learn from the tactics that perform there. You may recognize some of the lake or river traits I'm about to describe about these hot spots on your home water. If so, you can employ some of the same techniques and be confident that they'll perform on a waterway near you.

Like many of you, bass fishing and tournament fishing are hobbies and recreation for Karen Savik (I have a day job!), so the United States contains many excellent bass fisheries where I've never wetted a line! I'm looking forward to fishing and experiencing new water just like the readers of this book! A number of these destinations are in or near my home state of Minnesota, but that's where a good share of my fishing takes place. Again, I think the variability and learning opportunities of these lakes, rivers, and reservoirs are as important as the actual name.

Rainy Lake, Ontario, Canada

Let's start with one of the best: the Rainy Lake boundary water system on the northern border of Minnesota with Ontario. This body of water is part of a system of lakes and rivers that begin in the Boundary Waters Canoe Area Wilderness and extends through Rainy Lake, Rainy River, Lake of the Woods, and all the way up to Hudson Bay. In my experience, and in the experience of bass anglers who've been around longer than I have, Rainy Lake ranks as one of the top one or two smallmouth fisheries on Planet Earth. How's that for identifying good water?

At 345 square miles, this classic, glacially carved Canadian Shield lake qualifies as "big water" even by border country standards. In addition to smallmouth, Rainy contains a greatest hits of prime North American sportfish, including walleyes, northern pike, muskies, and lake trout. And you don't need a degree in fish biology to know that all that hard granite under the lake and exposed on its hundreds of islands is smallmouth heaven. The most difficult part about fishing Rainy's 220,000 acres is deciding where to start. Don't limit your search to the American side: The

Canadian Bass Championship occurs out of Fort Frances every year on the Maple Leaf side of Rainy Lake.

Rainy is special to me because I have friends who own a cabin on an island there. I've fished this beautiful, scenic wilderness lake many times. This is vacation country, so many rental cabins, houseboats, and other lodging options exist, too. I also will admit that it's the one waterway where I've actually eaten smallmouth. I felt terrible doing it, but hey, everyone has to try something once. Rainy is prime walleye water, so very few people are catching and eating bass here.

I've worked a lot of the 1,500 miles of shoreline on Rainy, including the Alexandria Bay area (thoroughly) many times and caught some huge smallies. There are many wonderful things about fishing Canadian water, and one is the fact that the fish seem a little dumber. When the lakes are covered by ice seven months out of the year (not to mention the relatively sparse human population of Canada), the fish simply see fewer lures—go figure. Consequently, they're more aggressive and are more likely to hit those big shiny lures that don't qualify as "finesse." Big hardware, like spinnerbaits, Mepps, and even spoons, has produced hefty bronzebacks for me on several occasions on Rainy. In a more traditional sense, you should also have tubes and grubs; bring lots of topwater lures, too. Though I've never done it, a number of guys swear by fly rods for Rainy Lake smallies, and it looks like a rip-roaring good time. Lake data from the Minnesota Department of Natural Resources showed the average smallmouth weighed in at over a pound. Battling a 4-pound smallie on a 5-weight rod while surrounded by North Country fall colors has got to be about as good as it gets for freshwater fishing. Trust me, you're in for a good time if you head to Rainy.

Lake Minnewashta, Minnesota

At 738 acres, Minnesota's Lake Minnewashta in Carver County (southwest of Minneapolis) may not strike most bassers as anything special. But this lake is near and dear to my heart for a number of reasons, partially because it's just twenty minutes from my day job and my home. I can buzz out there for a couple hours, then return for an afternoon shift. Sounds like a lake near you, too? That's the idea!

High points include decent water clarity of almost 14 feet and a sandy, mucky bottom that holds an abundance of healthy aquatic plant life. Minnesota's state record largemouth was caught in a very similar body of water nearby—Lake Auburn, in the same western Twin Cities metropolitan county. If you live in the eastern United Sates, you probably have a lake like Minnewashta near you.

When I first started fishing this lake, I worked almost exclusively a jig worm in some healthy cabbage beds. I could pull 5-pounders for hours. That was before the Eurasian water milfoil got bad; now (given the milfoil) I've switched to flipping with a jig-and-pig or Texas rig. That produces for the first half hour after locating a school, but then they just quit. You've probably been in this situation, too. I'd switch colors, then maybe pick up one more, then nothing.

A couple of my fishing buddies suggested that I get a 7-foot spinning rod with fluorocarbon leader and a good braided line, then work a ³⁄₁₆-ounce jig and worm and/or a finesse jig. So here's what I do now: When fish school after the spawn and head out to weed line for the recovery period in June, I look for turns, points, drops, and hard bottoms. Find all of them together, and you can fish all day. Later in summer, as the water heats up, I begin fishing deeper water; that's easy on Minnewashta because of the deep weed lines. There's an incognito breakline way off the eastern boat landing, and I love working the turn and tucks inside those weeds, especially if I can find a few rocks—that's my spot on a spot.

Minnewashta contains big bass, some increasingly large pike (ten years ago, the lake was notorious for hammerhandles, but that's slowly improving), and big bluegills—and it's a cute scenic little lake, to boot. Milfoil remains a problem for pleasure boaters and homeowners, although the controlled spraying for the exotic plant that occurs on the lake freaks me out more than the actual plant. Many bass anglers in North Country have simply accepted that you've got to work with the milfoil. On Minnewashta I shake a finesse jig (or a larger jig with a skirt or bit of trailer on it) a little, and the largies find it irresistible. Find those inside turns near deep water, maybe with some boulders atop a sandy bottom, and it will hold fish. Some guys call it deadsticking a lure: Just let it lie there, or barely move it. Bass can't stand it! As summer wears on, the bass will look for cover and shade. Then I spend a fair amount of time working docks or the lake's ample beds of lilies.

Sampling for bass was difficult in the past. The Minnesota Department of Natural Resources (DNR) uses gill nets and trap nets for much of its sampling, neither of which is very productive for bass, but the agency has been electrofishing Minnewashta in recent years. The results show largemouth in relatively good abundance levels and with above-average size. I can vouch for that! The average largemouth bass length was 14.2 inches; average weight was 1.7 pounds, with 15.2 percent of the bass sampled at over 18 inches. Thanks in part (or perhaps mostly) to a total catch-and-release regulation, Lake Minnewashta largies continue to sample bigger year after year.

A Carver County Regional Park provides some gorgeous green space, and that catch-and-release bass regulation on the lake keeps legions of meat anglers away. There are two public accesses on this fine lake.

Long Lake, Wisconsin

For a Minnesota girl, where the bass season usually doesn't open until Memorial Day, Wisconsin's early-May opener scratches the bassin' itch and gives me a chance to pursue some prespawn fish. At 3,300 acres, Long Lake (in northwestern Wisconsin's Washburn County) is known best as a premier walleye lake, but it also has good fishing for largemouth and smallmouth bass, northern pike, and crappies.

I have a soft spot for Long because it was the first lake that I fished as a professional angler, and I'll be honest with readers: I only caught one fish! The lake, however, has kept me coming back for more spring fishing. With its long, narrow shape (with loads of bays and other connected side lakes), Long contains an incredible amount of fine bass structure for such a relatively small body of water. From its northeast corner to its southernmost bay, Long probably doesn't stretch more than 9 miles, yet with all its twists and turns, it has nearly 100 miles of shoreline. We're in the heart of the Upper Midwest's prime walleye country here, and the DNR stocks that species extensively. But many multispecies anglers fish Long for walleyes and bass because strong, self-sustaining populations of our favorite fish live in this beautiful lake, too. A very approachable lake for new anglers, Long has many public accesses and easy-to-fish structure—plus smallies and largies in one place!

Long Lake is deep, with clear water and a lot of variety in its structure—rocky areas, sandy and gravel bars, weed beds, and a fair amount of natural woody cover. Most of the water in the lake falls within that perfect bassin' range between 5 and 20 feet. With all the wind-protected fishing locations, there are plenty of spots to fish relatively shallow bass, including around a couple of big islands. Like I said, I fish Long Lake early in the year (coldwater fishing) and have found success slowly retrieving jerkbaits for smallies. For largemouth, a jig-and-pig or a small ringworm with a little curly tail, fished slow and shallow, has produced well for me when dragging into the first breakline drop. Take your time, because these fish aren't too aggressive yet as they begin thinking spawn. I keep promising myself that I'll fish Long deeper into summer—rock piles farther out look great for postspawn smallies, and I've marked some creeks that would seem to hold largemouth later in the year, too.

As a tournament angler, I've always admired Long Lake because it's a body of water where you can win an event with big smallies or largemouth. Even in a largemouth lake in this part of the world, if there's rock, too, you're liable to find smallies. Wisconsin's Long Lake is a classic example. In most lakes containing both species, you're unlikely to find smallmouth large enough to boost your total weight into first place. On the contrary, that's very possible here, and it's a testament to the fine smallmouth fishing. With a Secchi disk reading of 12 feet, you can watch bass envelope your finesse rigs from quite a distance.

There are probably a dozen-plus Long lakes in Wisconsin (no kidding), but the one in southeastern Washburn County is in the beautiful vacation country north and slightly east of Rice Lake. Only a couple hours from the Twin Cities of Minnesota, the area offers great lodging with all the amenities.

Green Lake, Minnesota

Green Lake, in Minnesota's Kandiyohi County, has earned a reputation over the past decade as great smallmouth water. It's a lake worth highlighting here because it's an excellent bass fishery but also because it illustrates how anglers sometimes disagree over how to manage fisheries.

As part of some experimental regulations it was studying statewide, the

Minnesota DNR implemented catch-and-release only for all Green Lake bass in 1997. The timing was impeccable, thanks to some strong recent year-classes of smallies. Concern about bass eating young walleyes and affecting the forage base in this 5,406-acre central Minnesota lake caused a backlash among some walleye anglers. Eventually even the DNR said that the massive increase in smallmouth probably meant less forage, which could contribute to the decrease in the number of walleyes in Green. The walleye decrease in the agency's test nets *was* dramatic, although I think the clearer waters in Green (thanks to cleaning up of local septic lines and less farm runoff) helped boost the numbers of clean-water-loving smallies and drove the light-shy walleyes to deeper water.

Nonetheless, thanks to public pressure, the bass protections have come off the lake, first in 2001, when it went to a 14-inch maximum harvest, then a 14- to 21-inch protected slot in 2003. In 2006 it reverted to a statewide six-bass limit, although at least the smallmouth season lasts only a little over three months.

Even so, thanks to the catch-and-release culture so prevalent among bass anglers, and 11.5 miles of shoreline for bass to inhabit, Green will remain an awesome bass lake for a long time. The state's record smallmouth stands at an even 8 pounds, and other than Lake Mille Lacs, Green ranks as the most mentioned water that could produce the next record. Early this decade, 6-pound smallies were not uncommon in Green. During the Minnesota DNR's last survey, in 2005, the average smallie weighed 2.2 pounds and measured almost 16 inches!

The deep (110 feet), clear lake is full of rocky structure, and some people fish them with walleyelike rigs early in the season. Live bait tends to be a bit too lethal for my taste when fishing bass, so when I fished here in the fall, I stick with jigs or tubes in green, natural pumpkin colors. Also, I love drop-shotting this lake during a warm fall, when the fish become more aggressive. (Keep in mind that in Minnesota, "warm water" is a relative term.)

Green, perhaps more than any other bass fishing destination, has taught me the importance of working the edges and sides of submerged points rather than the top. There's a big underwater point on Green where I've focused on letting my lures fall on a slack line off the steep break. Do this and you'll be amazed at how often you get bite. Aquatic vegetation is generally limited in the lake, but some Eurasian water milfoil exists. Green

contains largemouth bass, but they run smaller than the bronzeback. There was, however, a big year-class of largemouth in 2002 that should be entering their bucketmouth years as the decade draws to a close.

Opposite: One of the author's favorite fall presentations on the bassy water of Minnesota's Green Lake is the drop-shot rig. For a description on how to set one up, see page 43.

West Okoboji, Iowa

Iowa's "Great Lakes" (no kidding) lie in northwestern part of the nation's top corn-producing state, and once were some of the most overlooked smallmouth water in the country. Located in Dickinson County, these glacial lakes are the largest natural lakes in the state. But Iowa for top bass fishing?

Thanks to a ton of magazine coverage during the past decade, the word is out on the fabulous bass fishing on West and East Lake Okoboji, Big Spirit, Minnewashta (Iowa), and Upper Gar. Seasoned fishing guides say these lakes rival any in North Country for consistent big smallmouth action, and if you know what you're doing, you can catch and release bronzebacks all day.

In Minnesota we sometimes joke about Iowa anglers being hard-core meat fishermen for everything, including bass. But the creel stats showing upwards of 90 percent release on Lake Okoboji don't bear that out. Like many lakes in this part of the country, there's a good profile of other "eating" fish like walleyes and panfish, so maybe that helps take pressure off bass. These are some prime, consistent smallmouth waters, and a fair number of tournaments arrive on Okoboji every year.

For the purposes of this section, I'll focus on West Okoboji—a 3,847-acre lake with a maximum depth of 136 feet. That makes it the deepest lake in Iowa and helps keep its waters cool in the middle of heartland farm country. Name the Midwestern sportfish— walleye, pike, muskie, or perch—and it probably swims in Okoboji. A piscatorial paradise, the lake produced the current Iowa record tiger muskie, northern pike, white bass, and the all-important smallmouth bass (a 7-pound, 12-ouncer in September 1990).

Thanks to a continuous bass season on most Iowa waters, I've fished Okoboji during the month of April several times. In my opinion, the smallmouth fishery is worth the hype, and it's a good largemouth lake, too. It's not an easy lake to fish, partially because of an abundance of structure, but I love a challenge!

Try fishing a tube or jig-and-pig for smallies in spring. Find any grass that you can early in the year and work it across the bottom. After the spawn, work deep water near any flats you can find on a lake map. You probably realize by now that smallies like rock points, rock piles, and reefs, and Okoboji contains all three. You can target bass via a number of presentations by working the edges of some large submerged reefs in this classic cool-water lake. Later in the year, work any rocks you mark along those deepwater transition zones. Okoboji has a reputation for small patches of weed beds that grow fairly deep—15 to 20 feet—and if you can correlate it to any rocky habitat, smallmouth love that combination.

It's also a great topwater lake, especially early or late in the open-water season, when bass are wearing the feedbag. I had an absolutely fabulous day throwing Zara Spooks one spring on Okoboji, and I've never recovered. One fabulous day like that can screw you up: It's all you ever want to cast!

Lake Vermilion, Minnesota

Lake Vermilion, in northeastern Minnesota's St. Louis County, lies within casting distance of the incredible Boundary Waters Canoe Area Wilderness and offers an unbeatable combination of scenic beauty and blue-ribbon bass water. Despite its remote setting, the 40,000-plus-acre Vermilion is very accessible and offers loads of quality lodging around the lake. With two very different basins of nearly equal size and a maximum depth of 76 feet, this North Country gem contains a variety of habitats that afford prime largemouth and smallmouth potential. Another glacially carved, Canadian Shield–type water, Lake Vermilion contains hundreds of reefs and boulder piles near drop-offs—ideal structure for smallmouth bass. Oak Narrows separates the two basins, and when I'm tournament fishing, I usually focus on one side.

The Minnesota DNR says that electrofishing catches of smallmouth bass have been relatively stable in recent years, after unusually high catches around the turn of the century. The lake produced strong year-classes of smallmouth bass in 1997, 1998, 2001, and 2002, so angling prospects for those mature age-classes are very good for the latter half of this decade. My experience suggests there are loads of smallies between 1 and 2 pounds, and a 6-pounder is more than possible.

Anglers pursuing largies usually work the shallow reeds near sandy bottom structure in the western basin. During summer, work spinnerbaits, topwater, and big crankbaits in these areas and near shorelines, even in very shallow water. Even though you're way north, Vermilion contains many shallow areas that heat up, so largies behave like their comrades farther south by taking shelter under docks, especially those adjacent to some vegetation. Unlike their southern cousins, however, they'll stay in these relatively cool shallow areas all season. Running Texas-rigged worms or tubes under docks is productive in many of the lake's bays. I've rarely fished largies on Vermilion, but when I have, those northern bays on the west side have been productive.

For smallies I've had good luck running medium-size crankbaits in natural colors over the breakline. It ranks as slightly tedious, at least until a 4-pound bronzeback bends your rod over! For smallies my boat heads first to the mouth of Pike's Bay in the southern portion (eastern basin) or Daisy Bay (west basin). In the eastern basin the islands near the town of Tower have a great reputation for producing big smallies. Don't be afraid to work docks on this side with tubes for bronzebacks, either. Later in summer, any areas where creeks or springs enter the lake and attract the cool water–loving smallmouth provide prime, fun opportunities for working topwater lures. Come fall, find rocky areas along the main lake shoreline or its dozens of islands where the water depth plunges quickly (the sheer-wall areas of border country contain a lot of these), and work deep-diving cranks. Don't be surprised if one of the lake's massive muskies (some believe it could produce Minnesota's next state record) follows or grabs your lure. Just prior to fall turnover, you'll have the time of your life working cranks or plastic grubs this way.

Finally, if you get really brave while staying in the Vermilion area, grab a canoe and try plying the waters of the nearby Boundary Waters Canoe Area Wilderness. It contains hundreds of lakes, many brimming with smallmouth that never hear the sound of a motorboat.

Mississippi River

The nation's largest river offers fine bass fishing for both species as it meanders south through the middle of the United States. Above the lock and dam system, upstream from the Twin Cities of Minneapolis/St. Paul, you'll find excellent smallmouth fishing in the free-running river. A fly-fishing-via-johnboat culture has even sprung to life there recently. For the purposes of this section, however, let's focus on the series of reservoir-like pools—compliments of the U.S. Army Corps of Engineers—that make up the Upper Mississippi from the Twin Cities to St. Louis. Millions of people live within casting distance of this great bass fishery.

This bass-lover doesn't exactly embrace heavy current with open arms, but you can't argue with the ability of current to create nifty little nooks and eddies that hold fish. A happy medium for me on the Mississippi is the slower-flow reservoir of Lake Pepin on the Minnesota-Wisconsin border. My typical smallmouth strategy focuses on notches or bulges along the shoreline—inevitably the downstream side will hold a bass or two. I cast a Carolina rig right up to the shoreline, then drag it back out. In slower current I'll even cast to the upstream side. Another technique capitalizes on the willingness of big bass to cruise the outskirts of cement culverts or bridges that abut the shoreline. Run a crankbait or virtually any rig adjacent to the cement, and it's amazing how often you'll hook a hawg.

Anywhere along the river, the fabulous wing dams hold multiple species of fish. These rocky underwater structures run at a slightly offset angle to the main Mississippi River channel to direct the bulk of the flow into the center. (As I stated earlier, in rivers—especially the Mississippi—you never know what you're going to catch!) I've had my best luck working the edges of the first or last wing dam in a series. Another good rule of thumb on the Mississippi River: Big river, smaller baits. Don't ask me why, but a smaller profile on any given lure produces more strikes for me on the Mighty Mississip'.

Now here's a contradiction for that last rule: Faster water, faster fish. You need to cover water on the Mississippi because even though the fish prefer smaller baits, they're aggressive and moving. Bass on the Mississippi River are some of the most aggressive fighting and striking fish in my part of the country. They're great fun, but don't expect to catch a whole school finesse-worming like you would in a lake scenario. In a river, everything is trying to eat everything else, so fish are on the move. You should be too.

Mississippi River bass run pretty shallow in my experience. (By the way, shore fishing opportunities abound on the Mississippi for that reason.) Along much of the upper reaches of this waterway, most anglers are pursuing walleyes or panfish, so despite the great opportunities, bass don't see much pressure beyond tournaments. Largemouth spawn in the shallow backwaters in spring, then chase forage in the thousands of minichannels between islands and other inlets off the main channel later in summer. Perhaps more so than on any other waterway, I find smallies and largies mingling on the Mississippi.

Lake Erie

Erie is the southernmost and shallowest of the Great Lakes, and although that's a poor combination for the trout and salmon many people associate with the Great Lakes, it creates a smorgasbord of bass habitat. When it comes to fishing incredibly big water like Lake Erie's 6.3 million acres, your initial search of a vast blue lakescape can be pretty daunting. Make it easy by focusing on bass habitats. When you begin eliminating unproductive, structureless water, you can hone in on obvious areas quickly.

Most of my Erie bassin' experience has occurred off the Ohio shoreline in the shallower, warmer Western Basin, which contains some of the lake's best smallmouth habitat. The islands area in the southeast corner and long, shallow reefs north of Port Clinton are especially good holding areas in spring. I've had my best luck simply drift-fishing these areas with tube baits or finesse rigs. The smallies typically have spawned by mid-May in the Western Basin (though later as you move east); postspawn they move to deep water off these spawning areas. As spring progresses to summer, the smallmouth head farther offshore to pursue forage off larger flats and reefs.

The exotic goby provides a top food source for Erie smallies, but they love crayfish, too. In summer you can mock the walleye anglers by front-trolling slowly over the edges of these offshore reefs with a tube or grub to mimic these baitfish.

Though Erie's smallmouth receive much of the press, this diverse fishery offers good largemouth fishing opportunities, too, and you can fish many of their locations just as you would on smaller bodies of water. The reefs near Port Clinton and Sandusky Bay will produce both species. Along the Pennsylvania shoreline near the city of Erie, Presque Isle Bay contains both species and calmer, flatter water for anglers who find the whole Great Lakes concept daunting. Unlike their brown cousins, who can disappear from an area quickly, the largie locations are more consistent and predictable. You can catch 2- to 4-pound largemouth all day with all the classic tactics, such as skipping Senkos or other soft baits under docks, or running spinnerbaits in the slack waters near any current—say, where a creek or culvert enters the big lake.

Since 2004 the season for all bass in the Ohio waters of Lake Erie closes from May 1 to June 29 to protect the spawning beds from nasty gobies, which will eat their eggs. Catch-and-release fishing is allowed, but do so quickly and ethically so that those bass can protect their beds and future generations of lunkers. Up the shore, in Pennsylvania and New York waters, slightly more liberal, one-over trophy regulations exist during spring spawning time. When fishing the extreme western portion of the lake, it's pretty easy to end up in Canadian waters. Make sure you know your position (some GPS chips don't include Canada structure), and be properly licensed. And expect big wind and big waves.

Anglers heading out on Lake Erie should possess a functional cell phone, a marine band radio, and commercial-grade lake maps showing reefs and other navigational hazards. Weather can change rapidly when you're fishing the tenth largest lake on Earth, and you need to be prepared to head to shore fast. Bring a healthy dose of common sense, too.

Lake Champlain, New York and Vermont

Ahhhhh, this is God's country—with a healthy dose of American history thrown in around Fort Ticonderoga and other historic sites. Though not a "great lake," so to speak, 278,000-acre (435-square-mile) Lake Champlain on the Vermont–New York (and Quebec) border contains excellent largemouth and smallmouth fisheries. Chalk that up to a variety of traits that bass love: clear water, rocky points and reefs, and abundant vegetation.

The sixth-largest lake in the United States, Champlain has more than seventy islands. At 400 feet deep, it stays cool enough for smallies (and other "cold water" species like Atlantic salmon and sturgeon), yet has plenty of shallow basins where largemouth reside. Lots of rocky islands offer fabulous structure, and a multitude of channels and current sources maintain a steady source of forage.

Other than the bays on the northeast side and South Bay on Champlain's southernmost tip, you can purchase a reciprocal fishing license that allows you fish the rest of the lake, whether it's Vermont or New York waters. In New York, all black bass fishing is strictly catch-and-release from December 1 through the second Saturday in June, and anglers must use artificial lures. Vermont also requires catch-and-release of all bass from about mid-April through early June.

I've fished both ends of Champlain and enjoyed great fishing everywhere on this lake. The southern end contains lots of milfoil, and I've caught largemouth in June by fishing tubes after the spawn. The fish had just moved out to the nearest and first weeds, which were fairly deep—say, 12 to 16 feet of water. Tournaments have brought me father north, to Plattsburgh, New York, where I've slammed the smallies via green spinnerbaits or crankbaits. Smallies on this lake also bang gold- and white-colored jerkbaits, especially in spring. Working the flats and points with these lures on windy days has been dynamite. On very windy days, mega-large Zara Spooks worked over the waves are ridiculously productive. Small ones work better on low-wind days; you can't beat topwater action like this for pure fun!

There are a couple specific places that I love on Champlain. On the north end (New York side), Windmill Point is a long, rocky finger that runs fairly shallow then dives deeper with a fair amount of grassy vegetation. Big cracks in the large underwater rocks harbor crayfish, and bass pursue them. To the right of Windmill, there's a big bay where I've found smallies roaming and swimming in schools—suspended almost like crappies. There are few weeds or other structure, so you have to search for them; but trust me, it's worth it. Like many bass havens, Champlain sees little serious pressure in the fall. Combine the gorgeous fall colors of the northeast United States with feedbag-wearing largemouth bass, and Champlain offers an impressive autumn fishery. Work late-summer and autumn smallmouth off deepwater reefs via crankbait, tubes, or grubs.

And, no, I've never seen Champy, the Loch Ness–like monster supposedly swimming Champlain's depths! Even if I had, it wouldn't keep me off this prime, beautiful chunk of bassin' water.

Thousand Islands, St. Lawrence River

The Thousand Islands region of the lower St. Lawrence River, where it borders New York and Ontario, contains excellent bass fishing and some unique international curiosities. Just like Minnesota has way more than 10,000 lakes, the Thousand Lakes Chain has way more than 1,000 islands—nearly 1,800 have some vegetation and remain above water year-round. The 50-mile chain straddles the Canada-U.S. border, and this gorgeous part of North America has been a vacation and resort destination in the Northeast for more than a century.

Let's see … loads of rocky island structure, light current carrying abundant baitfish, and cool water: Must be smallmouth country, so it's no surprise that Thousand Islands makes my top destination list (although the waterway contains healthy largemouth, too). The chain officially begins where the St. Lawrence River exits the eastern outlet of Lake Ontario, so you're near a tremendous cold-water fishery and many fine species of gamefish—from jumbo perch to muskies. There's lots of water here, and you need to focus on good structure, such as reefs and points that flare off all those islands and the shoreline, to target the bass.

This waterway contains some of the clearest water I've ever seen, partially because of—love 'em or hate 'em—zebra mussels. Viewing the bottom through such clear water 15 to 20 feet down borderline gives me vertigo, but it's remarkably beautiful. For your fishing purposes, it means these fish demand that you throw natural colors. My first mode of attack begins by throwing a weightless Senko near any island or shoal and letting it drop real slow. You'll find ample amounts of sea grass or turtle grass that holds mostly largemouth, and they must not see many wacky rigs, because they really slam this presentation during the postspawn period in June.

I've also had good luck here throwing spinnerbaits with green blades for smallmouth. In many areas you'll find patches of milfoil, and flipping these areas with a black-and-blue or green pumpkin jig has been a great second-wind technique in this waterway. You can fish the main river, where you'll obviously find more current—and more smallmouth—or work the backwater, lakelike portions. You could probably fish a lifetime for bass in the Thousand Islands region, but some prime areas that tournament anglers target include Lake of the Isles, Goose Bay, Chippewa Bay, and the

Admiralty Islands. I've fished a number of tournaments here, and it's one of my favorite North Country destinations.

Many scenic little towns and a bunch of state parks border the Thousands Islands region, so it's a great place to combine a love of bass fishing with a family vacation. You can enjoy great fishing for a few hours a day, then take advantage of the scenery, sights—including some remarkable architecture—and great restaurants with your spouse or family the remainder of the day. Rental boats and charters are available if you decide not to trailer your own watercraft.

Lake St. Clair, Michigan

Sometimes forgotten, given its proximity to its Great Lake cousins, St. Clair—at 430 square miles—still qualifies as big water. A border waterway between Michigan and the Province of Ontario, Lake St. Clair provides a connection to two Great Lakes: Lake Huron to the north and Lake Erie to the south. The St. Clair River connects the lake to Lake Huron, and the Detroit River connects it to Lake Erie. An extremely shallow lake with a maximum depth of 27 feet (maintained as part of the navigation channel), St. Clair contains relatively little structure compared to most of the waterways I've outlined in this chapter.

Yet despite that lack of classic structure that we bass anglers love, St. Clair contains something else we love even more: big bass. Chalk it up to all that cold Great Lakes water recharging the oxygen levels and dumping loads of baitfish into this narrow point in the Great Lakes hourglass, but something has maintained great bass fisheries in St. Clair. It also sports trophy walleyes, muskies, and other gamefish, which is perhaps why this mini–Great Lake receives a healthy dose of fishing pressure. Michigan protects spawning bass by allowing strictly catch-and-release fishing for the species from late April through mid-June.

Maybe it's the challenge of pursuing big bass in a tough fishing situation, but I've thoroughly enjoyed the tournaments that have brought me to Lake St. Clair. Successful anglers here bring two virtues: patience and a thorough understanding of their electronics. You'll spend time driving your boat and monitoring the bottom closely for any sort of rapid depth changes, dips, inside turns, or changes in substrate content. The smallies here are on the move, and you need to hunt for them. But don't waste too much time searching: When you find a ripple of structure, drift-fish it with a tube. If that's too much like walleye fishing for you, stick to throwing spinnerbait through the ample weed beds near shore and along the shipping channel for smallies.

Largemouth probably are underfished on this lake, but you can catch some impressive ones in Anchor Bay and in the back channels by working the vegetation or skipping docks with jigs or topwater. The communities on St. Clair's eastern shore, like Grosse Pointe, are some of the most upscale in the state, so you'll see some big docks and rigs around here. Nonetheless, this is a big, highly accessible lake that deserves its inclusion here.

Beaver Lake, Arkansas

With 483 miles of shoreline, this Ozark country lake offers a veritable theme park of bass-fishing opportunities. A reservoir behind Beaver Dam, which impounds the famed White River, Beaver Lake has 31,700 acres full of smallmouth, largemouth, and spotted bass. This northeastern Arkansas reservoir lies east of Bentonville—home of Wal-Mart—and the state has loads of recreational facilities surrounding the 50-mile-long waterway. There are plenty of private facilities, like rental cottages, and guides available, too. I love fishing this lake, and my first view of Beaver Lake each spring (I usually fish it in April) is one of my favorite moments of the year.

Because it's a reservoir, Beaver Lake contains some really deep water, and the turbidity level varies dramatically, from quite clear in the upper reaches to downright dark and fertile in the lower end. Given that, you're going to work for different species in different areas of the lake. There is a seemingly endless number of inlets, creeks, and shallow structure to work in this lake, too, so don't expect to learn it all in one weekend, or even a hundred weekends!

By now you've probably realized I'm a smallie-loving gal, so I'll often begin in the northern part of lake, where the clearer water provides better smallmouth habitat, plus a few of those smaller, albeit feisty, spotted bass. These are southern black bass, and this is about as far north as I've found them, but they're great fun! I'll work the gravel bars, clay bars, big underwater rocks, and all the different kinds of rocky shorelines. The U.S. Army Corps of Engineers created the dam and Beaver Lake in the early 1960s, so you'll still find flooded timber and stumps to work with hard baits. All will hold big, beautiful smallies.

Much of Beaver Lake qualifies as "advanced water" because it doesn't contain much natural structure or cover, so you better know how to use your electronics to find fish here. Study the bottom content, and work any transitions or areas with boulders or gravel first. By the time I arrive in late spring, the fish generally are sticking to transition zones or deeper water, though I'm told that earlier in the year, the smallies can run super shallow.

As you head upstream, the reservoir widens and begins to look more like a lake. As that turbidity increases, dig out the darker lures and spinners, and begin working the largemouth. I've fished the FLW tournament series on Beaver Lake and never done super well, perhaps because I focus too much on smallies. My rule on this lake is to go light, light, light. Seems like most guys who win tournaments here do it on the spotted bass, which demand finesse. Finally, though I focus on black bass, Beaver Lake also has a tremendous reputation for its striped bass fishery. One of these days, I'll have to target those fish, too.

Kentucky Lake, Kentucky and Tennessee

Another reservoir, Kentucky Lake comes to us compliments of the Tennessee Valley Authority, which dammed the Tennessee River back in the 1940s as part of that great public works era in American history. At 160,000-plus acres (51,000 in Kentucky), it's the largest man-made lake in the eastern United States, and it's chock-full of fishing opportunities along its 2,400 miles of shoreline. The lake and surrounding public lands, including a national wildlife refuge, state and county parks, and wildlife management areas, provide one of the biggest outdoor recreation regions in this part of the country. Another reservoir, Lake Barclay—an impoundment of the Cumberland River—lies to the east; a canal connects the two, both of which extend south into Tennessee. The peninsula between the reservoirs is the famed "Land Between the Lakes" national recreational area. At 180 miles long, Kentucky Lake offers a lifetime of fishing opportunities for multiple species, including largemouth and spotted bass, plus there's enough cool water to support a smallmouth fishery. (Combined with the long growing season, this lake produces some big smallies.) It's quite simply one of the top black bass fishing destinations in the world.

Because the TVA flooded areas with homes and farms to create Kentucky Lake, there are still buildings beneath the surface. I've fished the north end of each lake, and I prefer Kentucky Lake because it runs a little clearer and therefore contains more smallmouth, especially along the eastern shore. Barclay has a reputation for being a "numbers" lake, while Kentucky Lake seems to produce larger fish. Performing well in a tournament on Kentucky can be difficult, although I've had a lot of fun trying. There are just so many places to fish, including gravel bars on the main river, downed or flooded timber, and creek arms extending in so many different directions. I'm a kid in a candy store on this body of water.

In May when I've fished the lake for largies, I'll crankbait or Carolina rig the main points, and I almost always catch fish on the downriver side of those points unless there's very little current. (Water levels will fluctuate thank to the dams.) Usually I can't focus on weeds much because of the early time of year, but as summer progresses, healthy weed beds contain spotted bass and some of the nicest, healthiest largemouth I've ever encountered. Jump from creek to creek, and work the points and weed beds along them. Later in summer, when fish stick to the cooler, deeper water of the main lake channel, anglers targeting big bass will "stroke the jig" over the grassy center ledges of that channel. That technique is simple: Pull your jig up high, hard and fast, then let it drop back down. Be prepared to use your electronics to locate cool underwater seams and channels that will contain summertime bass. Later in summer, I'm told, spotted bass will behave almost like their white bass cousins and pursue schooling shad near the surface. Toss light-colored spinnerbaits or cranks, and you may just pick up a feisty "spot" on Kentucky Lake, too.

California Bassin' Opportunities

During the past couple of decades, California has earned a reputation as the Promised Land for trophy bass fishing. Though many of my friends have raved about great days on California water, I have yet to wet a line there—although I am planning to make time soon. The state's great reputation for clear-water finesse fishing opportunities appeals to me tremendously. Do a little research on potential trophy black bass waters in the United States, and it's amazing how many California reservoirs will make a Top-10 or Top-20 list. Though neither is native to the state, largemouth and smallmouth bass first were introduced to California in the late 1800s, and the big Florida largemouth subspecies was introduced in the 1950s. The long growing season and nutrient-rich reservoir waters in this part of the country mean the fish can grow large quickly, and anyone who knows anything about bass angling expects California eventually to produce the next world-record largie.

Northern California waters have produced most trophy-size smallmouth bass in the state, while big largemouth are found in waterways statewide. California's record largemouth weighed 21 pounds, 12 ounces, and was caught in Castaic Lake (Los Angeles County) in 1991. A Pardee Reservoir fish (Calaveras County—isn't that where that jumping frog came from?) set a new smallmouth record in July 2007 with a 9-pound, 13-ounce specimen. Both of those are impressive fish, wherever you're from!

California recognizes the number of visitors to the state who have a day or two of fishing opportunity, so it offers a nifty one- or two-day license for nonresident anglers. Got a day to burn during a business trip or after a visit to Disneyland? You can hit the water for bass as a nonresident for a measly $12.10, or two days for $18.65. Check the regulations closely for season openers and closures, however. Though much of the state's black bass water is open year-round, California (to its credit) recognizes that it's got a good thing going, so it has a pretty strong system of regulations establishing special seasons and size limitations.

The state has a strong tournament scene, a vibrant bass fishing club scene, and dozens of reservoirs stocked with America's favorite sportfish plus other black bass species, like spotted bass. A long state with a steep elevation gradient, California contains some diverse fisheries—from the tidal-influenced system of the Sacramento–San Joaquin Delta, to the warm impoundments within the state's southern and northern interior, to the cooler climate (and shorter growing season) of the Shasta Cascades.

The state's reputation for big bass has become borderline ridiculous, with people expecting 10-pounders on every other cast. Wherever you go, fishing is still fishing, and you may spend hours on a California reservoir and not catching anything larger than you did "back east."

Many believe that the next world-record bass might come from two of the state's most famous bodies of water in the southern portion of the state, Castaic and Casitas. There's an old saying that you can't catch a big fish if it doesn't exist. Well, they do exist in Castaic and Casistas, although getting them to strike is another matter. Many anglers are pursuing those fish, so they're conditioned to many lures (which is one reason they've gotten so big). Those lunkers won't respond to the same-old, same-old. My friend Tim Lesmeister wrote a piece in 2007 for *Outdoor News* explaining that the more successful California anglers are modifying, customizing, or creating new lures to entice those finicky California trophies. If you're not focused on 15-plus-pounders, however, you can throw standard equipment and catch nice bass by eastern U.S. standards all day. That's a good enough reason for me to head to the Golden State!

CHAPTER SEVEN

Twenty Tips and Tricks

While I was writing this book, a number of topics and concepts felt homeless—like they really didn't fit in anywhere. What follows are several tricks, idiosyncrasies, and nuances of fishing for bass (and fishing in general) that I've boiled down into twenty tips. Some address common questions I hear from newbie anglers. Any seasoned bass-chaser probably could fill another book with aha moments and specific techniques, but these simple ones will go a long way in improving your fishing and your understanding of this great sport.

1. **Keep a logbook.** As with any hobby, you'll improve your bass fishing by maintaining a log. Just a simple notebook where you jot down the date, weather conditions, hot lures or colors, GPS coordinates, and the habitat where you located fish will suffice. After a couple of years, that notebook will serve as a treasure chest of information for specific lakes you fish frequently, success stories, or bass habits in general. Yeah, we all have great memories, but trust me, you'll remember a lot more if you write them down!

Make sure to keep your log book waterproof with a zip-lock bag so you don't risk losing any of your valuable information.

2. **Odors.** All fish have a keen sense of smell, so foul or otherwise unnatural odors may turn them off, even if they're interested in the sight or sound of your bait. Rather than holding a lure long enough for you to set the hook, a bass will spit out or release a lure that tastes or smells unnatural within a couple of seconds. For that reason, wash your hands before you go fishing with an odor-free soap, and don't mess around with the gas or the tank the same day you're fishing. (Fill up the night before.) Finally, I keep a bottle of no-scent hand soap in my boat at all times.

3. **Fish attractants.** On a related topic, I use fish-attractant sprays and gels on most of my nonscented lures and recommend you do the same, sticking with natural or forage-based scents. Another trick: When rigging with tubes, insert a piece of cotton (that you've impregnated with scent) through the bottom, and push it to the top of the tube before rigging the hook. That way, the hook will help hold the cotton and scent in place much longer than if the cotton were farther down. You can do the same thing with a truly natural scent-producer: a chunk of crawler.

4. **Fish the rain.** OK, maybe I'm biased here, since I won my first professional event fishing in the rain! Predatory fish have an

advantage over preyfish in the rain, so even though conditions may be pretty miserable above the water, bass are feeding actively under it. Because of darker skies, combined with the turbulence at the top, preyfish can't see as well, and predatory fish take advantage of this by hunting hard. As I wrote earlier, light rain (or wind) creates a mild stirring effect that scatters potential food sources and energizes the bite. But too much of a good thing, that is, very heavy rain, slows the fishing. With all the incredible new clothing specifically designed for inclement weather, there's no reason you can't be comfortable when pursuing bass in such conditions. You're also likely to encounter less competition, go figure.

5. **Water level changes.** Here's a topic that river- or reservoir-fishing anglers (and lake anglers, too) face all too often. In general, rising water levels tend to drive bass into shallower water. Baitfish may have access to fresh food sources that previously were above water, and the predatory fish are following. Newly flooded vegetation, brush, or trees offer previously unavailable habitat and forage sources, so the bass want to tear it apart. A drop in water levels will drive fish, especially big bass, into deeper water. In general, fish don't like rapid changes to their environment, so a drop in water levels means they're trying to find a consistent (cooler) habitat. As you probably can tell, if I had to choose, I'd rather fish a rising-waters situation because it almost seems to stimulate the bite.

6. **Tool kit.** For making quick adjustments to your lures, keep a handy tool kit with scissors, small needlenose pliers, a pocketknife or multiuse tool, a file, and even some quick-drying glue on hand. If your top crankbait gets knocked out of tune in your tackle box and begins running erratically, you need the pliers to quickly bend the eye (right or left) where the line attaches. During tournaments, I'll often find myself adjusting jigs in a number of ways to alter the action— trimming skirts or trailers, cutting back the weed guard, or bending the hook for short strikers. Rather than constantly replacing "supersharp" hooks, buy quality hooks that—with your file—you can sharpen regularly. A sharp hook should

Opportunities to adjust lures present themselves constantly when fishing, and a simple tool kit will make your bass fishing lifestyle so much easier and enjoyable.

hang up on your fingernail as you drag it across. Fast-drying glue gives you the option of quickly adding a bead or rattle on any number of presentations.

7. **Changes in weather.** Rapidly rising or falling barometric pressure usually throws off the bass bite for twenty-four to forty-eight hours, especially in lakes. When this occurs, I generally focus on finesse offerings such as skirted jigs tossed in heavy vegetation. Bass become lethargic during those unstable hours immediately following a cold front, and they bite about

as lightly as you can imagine—when they bite at all. Avoid shallow water areas, where the effect seems more profound, and if possible fish areas with current, like rivers. Perhaps because river bass cope with an ever-changing environment, they can better handle weather-related issues and remain on the prowl.

8. **Stealth.** Some waters run clearer than others, so you need to take steps to avoid allowing fish to see you. Casting into the wind, though more awkward, can help you avoid spooking fish. Wind creates light current that carries forage, so predatory fish—like bass—often will face into the wind. If you can cast from behind them, you're reducing the odds they'll see your boat, plus your lure will be moving in the obvious direction of natural food sources. Again, try to cast well past obvious structure, and bring the lure to them looking as realistic as possible.

9. **Chasing birds**. In late summer, black bass will school and pursue baitfish, just like their white bass cousins. Feeding bass drive shad and other preyfish to the surface where gulls and terns will join the frenzy by diving at the surface. Hence the angling phrase "chasing birds." This tactic has worked for me while fishing just about anywhere in the country, especially on reservoirs down south or the Upper Mississippi River. Bites like this usually don't last long, but you can catch a bunch of fish quickly by casting natural-looking crankbaits, Rat-L-Traps, or swimjigs that match the color. For a tournament angler, this is like winning the lottery.

10. **Night fishing.** In urban areas that feature some phenomenal bass lakes—but also a lot of loud, intense public use during the daylight hours—night fishing offers the best time frame for catching big fish. Though it defies logic, you should stick with dark-colored lures, which will silhouette better at night. I usually start with dark-colored topwater lures at night but have caught good bass on just about every type of lure during this time. Two rules: Never fish alone, and make sure your boat is properly outfitted with lights (as required by law) before venturing out.

11. **Gear ratios.** Baitcaster gear ratios vary from about 4.1 to 7.1, and they're really very simple to understand. A 7.1:1 gear ratio on a baitcaster simply means that for every one 360-degree turn of the handle, the spool holding the line spins around seven times. Bottom line: The higher the ratio, the faster you can retrieve the lure. You usually want a fast ratio for presentations like spinnerbaits or buzzbaits, but stick with a lower gear ratio with finesse lures, like plastics. An angler would have a difficult time jigging a Texas rig, for example, slow enough on a 7.1:1 baitcaster. Fast retrieves move lures out of the strike zone too quickly, so it's good to have a low-ratioed baitcaster on one of your rods.

12. **Polarized sunglasses.** Want to make a great, and mandatory, fishing investment? By a pair of quality wraparound (or partially wraparound) polarized sunglasses. They serve several purposes—most important, in protecting your eyes. Keeping your eyes covered shields your gorgeous peepers from flying hooks, lures, or big insect (especially when you're running at full throttle). Polarized glass also protects your eyes better from damaging UV sunlight, plus you'll be squinting and straining your eyes less. Oh, and did I mention that polarizing sunglasses also allow you to see deeper into the water. When you're fishing, that's a good thing. Oh, here's a tip within a tip: Wear a hat—wide brim, baseball style, whatever—to keep the sun off your head and face and reduce glare.

13. **Lure color rules.** Here's a simple rule of thumb for rule selection: Dark day, dark lure; bright day, bright lure. Darker lures silhouette better when there's less ambient light, which could highlight yellow or white lures. In dark water during overcast days, black and blue jigs work great. This even applies for topwater lures—on an overcast day, I'll use a June bug or black skirt instead of a white skirt. The second part of this rule: The clearer the water, the more natural the color. Makes sense, right? If I'm flippin' a jig in clear water, that lure better look natural simply because fish can see it very well.

14. **Spook tip.** As you've read, you've probably noticed I'm a big fan of Zara Spooks and similar topwaters. One practical

problem I've found with these lures is that they lie level in the water, and sometimes bass will miss them on the strike. To up your odds, attach an adhesive weight strip to the back so that it dips down in the water a bit. Smallies love these lures and are less likely to miss when the lure hangs down a bit. Some tournament guys are cursing that I've given this tip away, but "Power to the people," I always say!

15. **All tied up.** Don't get too bogged down in knots. There are two easy ones I use almost exclusively: the Double-Uni knot for tying leaders to my main line and the Palomar knot for tying on my lures. The superstrong Double-Uni works great for joining two lines of similar or different diameters or materials. Some say the Palomar knot leaves too much tag-end waste, but it's quick to tie with great strength, and it's easy even for beginners. Check both regularly to ensure they're tight and not fraying or weakening.

16. **Fishing Line 101.** Two quick line rules of thumb: First, always check your line, especially monofilament, for nicks or cuts; and replace it regularly. Also, avoid cheap line that retains memory. Such line won't cast as far, plus it won't allow your lure to act natural in the water. Also, line that's ridiculously heavy or ridiculously light for your lure poses problems. The former doesn't allow your lure to deliver its best action; the latter sets up a situation where a lunker fish could break your line.

    Now here's my lineup, so to speak. All my spinning rods have braided line with a fluorocarbon leader. The braided line provides great sensitivity for subtle bites while finesse rigging and jigging, and the leader delivers reduced line visibility at the lure. (Braided line is less likely to tangle, a big pet peeve of mine when using spinning gear.) I change the line-test of the leader depending on the cover. In gin-clear water, such as at an event I fished during spring 2007 in Arkansas, I fished six-pound fluorocarbon while working a little jighead around trees. Yes, I risked breaking that smaller diameter line, but if you don't hook fish because your line is too obnoxious, you have no chance. My baitcasters have monofilament, and I usually start with twelve-pound test because it casts nicely, and

Opposite: Adding a red treble to the front of a crankbait adds some gill-flash realism to the lure.

that test weight allows lures to dive to adequate depths. If I want my cranks to dive deeper, I may switch to ten-pound test; if I'm casting spinnerbaits or swimming jigs in thick cover or rocks, I'll increase it to fifteen-pound test.

17. **Topwater tip**. The number one most important thing with topwater: Wait to set the hook. Don't set it until the lure is gone and you feel the strike in the handle. Then pause, take up the slack, and send your rod tip skyward. And if bass miss the lure (or you miss the hookset) on the first strike, don't stop reeling. Keep the lure moving. Give Billy Bass an opportunity to study a stationary artificial lure, and he may decide not to strike again.

18. **Red hooks.** Some anglers swear by red hooks 24/7, believing they simulate the red gill or blood on a wounded baitfish. Though I'll occasionally use them on drop-shot rigs, I mostly use red trebles on my crankbaits' front hook. Crankbaits are running fast, and a lot of pros believe that red up front mimics a gill flash. Try them, especially on fast-swimming crankbaits. One caveat: Any time you change hooks on a lure, cast it out for a test run to double-check the action. Hooks significantly lighter or heavier than appropriate for a lure, especially cranks, can disrupt its wobble.

19. **Marker buoys.** It's easy to drift away and lose your bearings, so when you catch a bass while search-fishing, toss out a marker buoy. To avoid working too much marginal bass habitat, I'll sometimes drift a point without casting and drop two buoys—one over a good-looking inside turn and another where the point ends (a natural crossroads with lots of fish movement). Then I'll target those two spots fast and dirty. Deep water, where there are few natural lakeshore objects to align your location, is a logical place to drop a marker buoy. When you catch a fish in weeds, sometimes torn-up, floating vegetation can serve as a natural marker buoy if you want to be discreet and not alert other anglers to your spot.

20. **Landing bass.** Neither smallmouth nor largemouth bass have teeth, so many regular bass anglers "lip" their bass by hand when landing them. Paying attention to the hook(s) on your

A quick release will ensure that future generations of anglers can enjoy the same quality of bass fishing that we can take for granted today.

lure, you simply pinch the lower jaw between your thumb and index finger, then lift. This temporarily paralyzes all bass and gives you the opportunity for a quick photo and release or a safe deposit in a live well. With really big fish, their body weight can put a lot of pressure on them during lipping, so you may want to place one hand under your catch's belly. I avoid nets when fishing for fun because anything that touches a fish's body can remove its important slime layer and decrease its chances of survival after release. Try to handle them with wet hands.

CHAPTER EIGHT

Building the Next Generation of Bassers

During 2007 as the U.S. Fish and Wildlife Service released its state-by-state reports on hunting and fishing trends, we saw some sobering headlines. The number of people participating in these sports continues to show a gradual decline, and among young people—especially tweeners and young adults—we're seeing growing disinterest in the natural world.

As the parent of two young women, I can partially understand how that's happened. Kids have so many outlets these days that I never dreamed about as a youngster. Plasma TVs, hundreds of cable channels, the Internet, Xboxes, year-round sports, music, dance—all that's just the tip of the iceberg. Throw in the growing access problems for modern hunters, and it's easy to see why the shooting sports are suffering the loss in participants. But you know what, folks? Fishing doesn't have that problem. The water in America belongs to all people, and it's rarely inaccessible to anyone.

Nonetheless, the decline in the numbers of young people heading out of doors is scary for many reasons. It troubles me because, as I said in the introduction, I want to share the wonderful world of fishing with

more people. Fishing license fees and the excise taxes we pay on fishing equipment fund a good share of the stocking programs and fish habitat improvement that occurs all across the country. Even people who never step outside benefit from these expenditures, via a healthier environment. But if the next generation doesn't step up and become active in the fishing sports, who's going to fund all that? Where will the next generation of tournament pros come from?

There's an answer and it involves each of us taking the time to introduce a kid to fishing. Many of us have encountered those situations where we're planning a multi-hour trip with children, and after fifteen minutes, the kid or kids are whining: "We're bored! We want to go home!" Wrong approach, obviously.

So how do we keep kids interested in what we're doing so they remain participants for life? Well, I can't promise that, but I can throw out some ideas that should at least keep them from driving you, their loving mentor, nuts for a couple of hours.

Fishing with Kids Do's and Don'ts

Do bring live bait. Normally, I'm not a big fan of using live bait, especially for bass, but when fishing with young kids, I make an exception. Fish are more likely to gut-hook themselves with live bait, and that makes successful catch-and-release more difficult, because that fish is just less likely to survive. But the simple fact is that you're going to get more action using live bait, and action is what kids demand.

When the fish aren't biting, some curious little kids can occupy themselves for hours by poking and prodding the minnow bucket or worm container. As adults, our gut instinct is to bark, "Get out of there!" but avoid that temptation. Explain what you're using for live bait, why it's effective, and where the bait came from. Kids ask questions you probably won't know the answers to yourself, but by discovering responses for them, you might just become a better angler yourself.

Do mix it up. I remember sitting in on one of my daughter's kindergarten or preschool classes years ago. Besides being utterly amazed at the patience those teachers displayed, I noticed a method to their madness. They rarely focused on any one task for more than twenty minutes before switching

Opposite: Before teaching kids the intricacies of bass fishing, help them develop a love for fishing in general with some time at the local panfishing hole.

to something new. Kids by their nature have short attention spans, and—I don't care if you're a former Marine Corps drill instructor—we're never going to change that, so don't try. Teachers understand that fact, and we should, too. So instead of taking a kid backtrolling for walleyes for hours, work on mixing up your tactics. Bobber fish for a little while. Bass aren't shy about taking the occasional worm on a hook. Then try casting a crankbait or spinnerbait. That not working? Show them how to wacky rig or drag a Texas Rig across the bottom. These aren't difficult techniques for 8- or 9-year-olds.

While you're helping them with their technique, keep your line in the water, too, so you can maximize the potential for fish. Keep it simple and do something low maintenance like placing a big sucker minnow under a bobber and letting it sit. You can focus on the kids, not your line, and if something takes your minnow—maybe a bass or larger pike—you and your young companion will have lots of fun playing the fish.

I know this is a bass fishing book, but kids don't care what they catch. Think about that before you head out. Those lake reports I suggested that you use as research tools? Use them now to ensure you're taking kids to a lake with multiple species of fish. They love variety, so don't take them to some mudhole filled with nothing but carp and bullhead. (That's not to diss roughfish, which can put up an awesome fight. Kids don't care what they're catching, so be upbeat no matter what's biting, even if it is an ugly carp.)

Consider which species you're targeting and how you're targeting it. One parent lamented to me that his kid was really crabby after two hours of trolling for lake trout from a canoe. Let's see, trolling for two hours in a canoe with no bites. I'm not sure I could handle that! They call muskies the "fish of 10,000 casts," so that's probably not the species to target with a new angler, either, eh?

Every list of kid fishing recommendations suggests working the bluegills and sunnies. That's a great place to start, however, everyone—doesn't matter what the age—gets sick of catching 3-inch bluegills after thirty minutes. I can think of no species that offers a more logical next step than the bountiful bass we've described in this book! Kids love the word "bass"!

Do be willing to move. Not only should you be prepared to change the species you're targeting, but if possible, change fishing spots frequently, too.

I've had some fishing trips (with adult newbies and kids alike) transform into boat tours, and that's OK, because everyone likes seeing new places.

Don't discount the brainpower of a little kid. Talk a lot about the species of fish you're pursuing while they're fishing. I know a 5-year-old who almost drives his parents nuts talking about fish, and he can recite some facts about "salmonids" and "the bass family" (no kidding) that many adult fishermen don't know.

While fishing, engage their brains in ways beyond constant physical stimulation. When you're switching lures or rods, explain why you're doing it. They may not absorb every fact you throw out during conversation, but even if a small percentage of it sticks, you're that much closer to building a fishing partner for life.

Do focus on the child. Another fishing (or hunting) rule when out-of-doors with youngsters: Make the child the focus of the attention. I've seen too many parents focusing on themselves and their recreational success. If that's your goal, more power to you, but leave the kids at home. Both of you are going to end up frustrated and angry if you're focused on yourself and not the high-maintenance-by-nature kid. This is their time to ask 1.2 billion questions and be ridiculously persistent without you becoming impatient.

Do pre-rig as much of your tackle as possible before hitting the water. The less downtime with kids, the better.

Do bring food, lots of it. Yes, I know there's an obesity problem in America, so bring a cooler with healthful snacks, like raisins, fruit, kiddie sandwiches, yogurt, whatever. When the whining pushes you to your breaking point, give them some food. It might just calm them down until the fishing action picks up.

Do keep trips short and sweet by choosing nearby waterways for your initial trips. Nothing's worse than crabby kids already worn out from an epic drive before you even wet a line. Mom-and-pop family-oriented resorts (which sadly are becoming harder to find) are great places to expose kids to fishing. Help them the first time or two to get set up, then let them do it themselves and learn from their own mistakes.

Don't go out-of-doors unprepared. Take it from a gal who's spent thousands of hours recreating on the water: The outdoors can be pretty unforgiving. Try to choose weather and an all-around environment that will provide youngsters with a good experience. You can help by setting off well-prepared with lots of sunscreen, bug dope, and functional clothing starting with a good cap.

Do use decent equipment. Many people recommend using spincast equipment for kids. That's fine, though I've had as much luck using spinning reels with kids. My only advice here would be to purchase mid-quality equipment (and line) that's less prone to tangles and hang-ups.

You'll fuel the anticipation if the child has his or her own equipment. It just puts a little more ownership into the whole experience. That said, I recognize that not every child or parent can afford decent equipment, but here's some advice I offered some low-income kids and parents at a children's seminar I gave last year: Take a couple kids to a boat landing with a nearby fishing pier or dock where you can fish. (Such spots usually have portable toilets, which the kids will appreciate.) Have the kids bring a five-gallon bucket with a sponge or two and load them down with drinks and sweets. Throw a bag of ice on top if needed. As boats leave the lake, the kids can ask if the owner would be willing to part with a couple bucks to have their boats scrubbed down. (In Minnesota, we're required to scrutinize our boats when they come off the lake to ensure that we're not transporting Eurasian water milfoil.)

Take it from a professional angler who's scrubbed down more than her fair share of boats over the years: I'd love to pay a couple of hard-working kids $5 to give my boat a quick once-over now and then. On a busy weekend day, a kid could make more than enough to buy him- or herself a fine rod-and-reel combo to enjoy many years of fishing.

At the end of the day, make sure the kids pick up all their trash, and encourage youngsters to leave the out-of-doors better than they found it. Throw the trash in that bucket, and toss it all out in the proper receptacle on your way home.

As for tackle, simple lures to keep in their own tackle box include beetle spins, crankbaits, spinnerbaits, and a Senko. That latter is super easy to wacky rig, and it will clean up on bass of all sizes. With hardbaits, kids will cast their brains out, so buy some inexpensive styles in case they get snagged and break off.

Do be safe. It should go without saying, but it bears repeating: Make sure the kids are wearing their life jackets, and set a good example by wearing yours, too.

Do practice conservation. In my experience, kids take to catch-and-release better than most older folks. They love to watch a fish disappear with a flick of its tail and the promise to be caught again another day. If you catch bass, show kids how to lip them, and snap pictures quickly. Explain that a fish is holding its breath whenever it's not in the water.

Do keep some small fish to eat. Keeping a few bluegills and sunnies, then step-by-step cleaning and cooking the fish is a process kids enjoy and gives them a better understanding and respect for the fish and their food in general. And it's like the old saying, "Teach a person to fish, and he'll never go hungry!"

Finally, if you're an adult and personally disinterested in fishing, look into any programs your state natural resources agency may have for exposing youth to fishing. My home state, Minnesota, has the MinnAqua program that has introduced thousands of kids to safe, affordable, and successful fishing via fun clinics at easy-to-access water.

My kids still fish with me and a highlight of my tournament career was the time my daughter Britta partnered an event with me and caught the most fish in our boat!

I'll leave you with this story. A professional angling friend of mine wanted desperately for his son to join him as an amateur angler on a pro tour. The kid took to the competition and all-day fishing like a postspawn bass to a breakline. Now my friend complains that he doesn't fish enough anymore because his son is constantly "borrowing" his boat!

Be careful teaching kids to fish: You might just create an angling monster! What a great problem to have.

CHAPTER NINE

Closing Thoughts

From a closing thoughts perspective, I'd like to restate something from the very beginning of this book: Bass belong to all of us. Americans sometimes take the concept of public waters for granted. We shouldn't, because there are many other places in the word where rank-and-file citizens of all economic backgrounds can't access lakes, rivers, and streams. Early in our country's founding, We the People decided that the citizens would own the waters of this land, and that's created one of the most recreational fishing–oriented cultures on the planet. I feel privileged to live in a nation with such opportunities, and I consider it one of many subtle freedoms and gifts too many people forget they have.

That gift carries responsibility. One of the greatest aspects of fishing is enjoying the sights and sounds of the great outdoors: Songbirds on the shore, raptors soaring overhead, maybe a doe and fawn sneaking a drink while your trolling motor almost silently glides your boat past on a foggy spring morning. A moment like that feels almost spiritual to me. America is beautiful, and it's up to us to keep it that way. Pick up after yourself and other people, too. Tournament and nontournament anglers alike are representing fishing, so let's set a great example for our kids (and other adults, too) when we're on the water.

Now I'm not going to suggest we replace the bald eagle as our national symbol, but if there's a fish that represents America best, it's the bass. She's tough, muscular, defiant, happy to brawl when necessary, yet semisocial, even gregarious. She demands a clean environment, but she's a survivor, too, and has found ways to thrive in the entire Lower 48. Largemouth and smallmouth bass are the common woman's (or man's) fish, and anyone with a fishing rod and a little knowledge can pursue this incredible species.

You've got the knowledge—now go get 'em!

INDEX

Born and raised in Minnesota, Karen Savik bought her first boat in 1991 and began tournament bass fishing in 1994. She turned pro in 1996 and fished the entire Minnesota-based Silverado Pro-Am circuit that year. Savik made history with her first tournament victory, which occurred in difficult downpour conditions at the Minneapolis Aquatennial Bass Championship in July 1997. With the win she became the first woman in Minnesota to win a professional bass tournament. She told *Outdoor News* at the time, "I was fishing against the best and never thought I would come in with a bigger bag of fish than them!"

Since then, Savik has focused on the national bass tournament trails, and for most of this decade, she has fished the FLW bass tour. In 2001 she became the first woman to qualify for the Everstart series national championship and finished the year in fifteenth place overall. Savik has remained competitive ever since, and she completed this book while on the road fishing the FLW tour during spring 2007.

In addition to being a pro angler for half the year and running a part-time bass fishing guide service on Minnesota's world-famous Lake Minnetonka, Savik owns and operates a restaurant with her husband of twenty-seven years, Ken, in Wayzata, Minnesota. The Saviks live in St. Louis Park, Minnesota, and have two daughters, Britta and Kirsten.

Get more secrets from the pros in these fine Pro Tactics™ books:

Pro Tactics™: Catfish

Pro Tactics™: How to Fish Bass Tournaments

Pro Tactics™: How to Fish Walleye Tournaments

Pro Tactics™: Ice Fishing

Pro Tactics™: Muskie

Pro Tactics™: Northern Pike

Pro Tactics™: Panfish

Pro Tactics™: Steelhead & Salmon

Pro Tactics™: Tackle Repair & Maintenance

Pro Tactics™: The Fishing Boat

Pro Tactics™: Walleye